ZEN AND THE
GOSPEL OF THOMAS

T0115590

ZEN AND THE GOSPEL OF THOMAS

JOANNE P. MILLER

Wisdom Publications
199 Elm Street
Somerville, MA 02144 USA
wisdompubs.org

Library of Congress Cataloging-in-Publication Data
Names: Miller, Joanne P., author.
Title: Zen and the Gospel of Thomas / Joanne P. Miller.
Description: Somerville, MA: Wisdom Publications,
    2018. | Includes bibliographical references. |
Identifiers: LCCN 2017037688 (print) | LCCN 2018000077 (ebook) |
    ISBN 9781614293811 (ebook) | ISBN 9781614293651 (paperback)
Subjects: LCSH: Gospel of Thomas (Coptic Gospel)—Criticism,
    interpretation, etc. | Koan. | Christianity and other religions—Zen
    Buddhism. | Zen Buddhism—Relations—Christianity. | BISAC:
    RELIGION / Buddhism / Zen (see also PHILOSOPHY / Zen). |
    RELIGION / Comparative Religion. | RELIGION / Gnosticism.
Classification: LCC BS2860.T52 (ebook) | LCC BS2860.
    T52 M535 2018 (print) | DDC 229/.8—dc23
LC record available at https://lccn.loc.gov/2017037688

ISBN 978-1-61429-365-1   ebook ISBN 978-1-61429-381-1

22 21 20 19 18
5 4 3 2 1

Cover design by Jim Zaccaria. Interior design by Kristin
Goble. Set in Adoble Garamond Pro 11/16.

Wisdom Publications' books are printed on acid-free paper and meet the
guidelines for permanence and durability of the Production Guidelines
for Book Longevity of the Council on Library Resources.

✪This book was produced with environmental mindfulness. For more
information, please visit wisdompubs.org/wisdom-environment.

Printed in the United States of America.

Please visit fscus.org.

I dedicate this to my community the Mountain Moon Zen Society in thanks for the compassionate guidance of my teachers Zen Master Roselyn Stone (Seiun An Roshi) and Zen Master Li-yea Bretz (also called Seiun An Roshi). And of course, to the old Buddha himself. Truly, the matriarchs and ancestors of Zen have not deceived me.

CONTENTS

PREFACE

The late Marcus Borg—New Testament scholar, theologian, and author—once made the observation that if Jesus and the Buddha were to meet they would recognize each other. I think the *Gospel of Thomas* is proof of that.

Imagine that the Buddha asked Jesus to write a text for a Zen audience that would explain his take on the mysteries of his Kingdom. Imagine also that Jesus chose to present it in a set of short koanlike sayings similar to the classic koan collections of the Zen tradition. In a way, this is how I read the *Gospel of Thomas*.

In *Thomas* I immediately recognize a kindred spirit. I am drawn to savor each saying as I would a koan in my own tradition—sitting with it, letting it sink into the marrow of my bones until a personal and individual understanding arises. The more I read *Thomas,* the more I feel it resonates deeply with my own koan practice, and the more delighted I am by the two traditions' synchronicity.

Thomas is an unusual text. It is readily apparent to anyone who reads it that it has an Eastern feel, that its Jesus is manifesting as the wisdom teacher, the one who has not come to tell us what wisdom *is* but to inspire us to develop it in ourselves. Like Buddha, this Jesus wishes us to realize, individually and personally, the truth of the eternal. A Zen reading of the *Gospel of Thomas* allows us to access the living Jesus through Buddhist eyes so we can add to and refine our own practice with his wisdom. Likewise, *Thomas* can be a gateway for Christians to make use of Zen.

In this book, I begin each chapter with a numbered saying (sometimes called a *logion*) from the *Gospel of Thomas* and quotation from somewhere within the Zen or larger Buddhist canon that I feel resonates with it. For me, when I read *Thomas* such parallels rise rapidly and frequently to mind. This is not a case of finding what "matches" in Zen and Christianity or of rewriting Christian doctrine for Zen Buddhists. To my great delight, they just naturally prompt an understanding completely at home within my tradition, and this understanding automatically connects them to a wide variety of Buddhist texts and themes. And then in the body of each chapter I comment on those themes.

For those not familiar with the *Gospel of Thomas* or the Gnostic gospels generally, *Thomas* is considered a part of the apocrypha—a noncanonical collection of ancient books, contemporaneous with much of the canonical Bible, that are not a part of orthodox Christianity but nevertheless are often considered inspired and deserving of a place in the canon.

Thomas (not to be confused with the *Infancy Gospel of Thomas*, which is about the childhood of Jesus) is perhaps the most famous manuscript discovery of the last century. It is a Coptic manuscript discovered in 1945 at Nag Hammadi in Egypt. Before this, very little was known about it other than three small fragments that date to 200 C.E. Some scholars lean toward seeing *Thomas* as a more primitive version of Jesus's original sayings, while others view it as a later gospel written after 140 C.E.

While it is usually considered a Gnostic gospel, the consensus is that it is not actually Gnostic in a certain technical sense. *Gnosticism* is a collection of ancient religions whose adherents rejected the material world and embraced the spiritual world. The teachings in *Thomas*, however, are for the *whole* of our lives in this present moment. In the main I have taken these teachings from Mark M. Mattison's *Gospel of Thomas: A Public Domain Translation*. One or two sayings have been taken from *The Gospel of Thomas: The Gnostic Wisdom of Jesus* by Jean-Yves Leloup,

The Coptic Gospel of Thomas by Beate Blatz, and Lynn Bauman's *The Gospel of Thomas: Wisdom of the Twin*. The Amplified Bible and the New Revised Standard Version Bible provided Bible passages.

Thomas has a short preamble and 114 separate sayings. The majority of these begin with "Jesus said," much in the same way that many early Buddhist suttas begin with "Thus I have heard." Like Ananda, who remembered the Buddha's words for posterity, *Thomas*'s prologue tells us that a follower of Jesus called Didymos Judas Thomas (neither Saint Thomas the Apostle nor Judas Iscariot) will tell us the "secret sayings" of Jesus.

These short sayings are thus a kind of a *hadith* of Jesus. In Islam, a hadith is a traditional account of things said or done by Muhammad or his companions. Unlike the New Testament, however, these teachings are given without context or narrative. It is this feature that makes *Thomas* appear koanlike.

While many of the sayings have parallels in the four canonical Gospels, they are sometimes sparser, sometimes larger, and often worded differently. All of them challenge us to break out of our intellectual impasse and intuit wisdom. As with Zen koans, the meaning of some sayings seems immediately apparent, while others require careful and prolonged contemplation. The koans that appear in this book are from the authorized Sanbo-Zen koan curriculum while other sutra excerpts were drawn from two public domain sources: Mettanet-Lanka's *The Tipitaka* and The Internet Sacred Text Archive *Buddhism* homepage.

For those readers who are not familiar with koans, perhaps an explanation of them is also needed at this point. In Zen Buddhism a student can be given a set of koans to work with in order to sharpen and mature their insight. Koans are short pieces of text usually in the form of a story, dialogue, question, or statement concerning a certain theme or understanding to be made clear. The purpose of a koan is to tell you about yourself—just as the sayings of the *Gospel of Thomas* do.

The unfortunate thing about koans is that they have, in some quarters, somehow acquired the unsavory reputation of either being riddles or nonsensical paradoxes, designed to somehow completely eliminate the intellectual mind. Some people are afraid of koans precisely because of this—and yet once we dive right into them we realize that they are in a certain sense actually the most straightforward and simplest of things.

So how do we embody koans? How do we come to know them? We read the koan first, letting it sink and settle into us. We do not begin by analyzing it. Sometimes a word or feeling stands out, and if so, we sit with that. We just sit with whatever comes up without intellectually dissecting it or expecting anything at all to happen or to stop happening. We may repeat a word with the breath or come back to a particular feeling from time to time. If we do that, the only thing we are doing is breathing that word and feeling that feeling. Some traditions have students jot down anything that comes to mind in this process—as I myself did with *Thomas*—and others don't.

The amazing thing about working in this way is that eventually out of nowhere the meaning becomes apparent. At a time—appointed by the koan, and not by ourselves—the meaning shows itself to you. As for why or when this happens, I can't pin the mechanism down to just one thing or one time frame. All I know is that koans have taught me to completely trust in what Buddhists in Japan call *myoshi*, "mysterious guidance" or "incomprehensible assistance"—the ever-present compassion that functions in emptiness. This universe wants us to wake up, and koans help us do precisely that.

Like koans, the sayings in the *Gospel of Thomas* ask each of us to discover the same secrets of mystery that Jesus himself discovered and to live out that knowledge in our own unique way.

I first dove deeply into *Thomas* during chemotherapy for cancer. As you can imagine, it captivated me from the very first line—"Whoever penetrates the meaning of these words will not taste death." My hope is that this book engenders in its readers some of the same sorts of discoveries I myself have had through seeing *Thomas* with Zen eyes.

1

PROLOGUE: THE SECRETS OF MYSTERY

These are the hidden sayings that the living Jesus spoke and
Didymos Judas Thomas wrote down.

—Gospel of Thomas, prologue

The Dharma is profound, difficult to realize, hard to understand, tranquilizing, sweet, not to be grasped by mere logic,
subtle, comprehensible only by the wise.

—Digha Nikaya (1.28)

There are two key phrases in the Prologue of *Thomas*—"secret sayings" (or "hidden sayings") and the "living Jesus." The first refers to
the nature of the search that this gospel encourages and the second to the
type of life that wisdom produces.

When it came to secret meanings and secrecy in general, the
Buddha had strong reservations and actively spoke against what he
called the "closed fist" of a teacher who holds something essential back.
He practiced and encouraged complete transparency in his teaching.
To keep secret something that might help others was unthinkable to
him—the mark of a false teacher. I think the Jesus in *Thomas* would
agree with him.

Yet closed-fist secrecy is not the only type of secrecy there is. Sometimes *secret* can simply point to a nonconceptual, meditative style and method of encouraging insight of direct experience—and this kind of secrecy is in no way the mystical world's equivalent of a conspiracy. Sometimes *secret* may merely refer to the mystery of the ultimate. Zen Buddhists will tell you that the eternal is unknown and indescribable except by means of intuitive realization that delivers knowledge outside of words and concepts. For this reason we don't always see it at first glance—even though it is, in a sense, hidden in plain sight.

The closed fist of withholding knowledge does not appear in the *Gospel of Thomas*, even though many of the sayings appear completely unfathomable at first glance. The sayings don't deny us anything, and they don't hold anything back at all—and yet they do need effort and insight to be understood. In fact, what may seem like a closed fist in *Thomas* is more akin to what is known in Zen as a *gateless gate*, the barrier of the ancestors. The gateless gate is the checking mechanism by which ancient Zen masters ascertained whether their students were really realized or were merely aping Zen and mouthing the sutras.

This barrier is really no barrier, and there is of course no actual gate—but we imagine there is because we're caught up in intellectualization and concepts. The gate is *us*, or more specifically, our sense of being separate from everything around us. When we realize this is not true, then we know the "hidden" secrets for ourselves. When we have gone through the barrier, an old Zen saying goes, we will walk freely between heaven and earth.

The secret sayings of Jesus require us to approach each saying as something to savor and sit with, to contemplate and meditate upon until our understanding matures most fully.

Given the effort to realize mystery, we can also see that in one way *secret* can in fact mean knowledge confined to and understandable only by a small group of people. This is for a practical and simple reason—not many people are willing to travel the difficult road to understanding in the method suggested by *Thomas*. It just isn't everyone's cup of tea. For me Zen is plain and simple, and very practical—but to others it can seem obscure, overly rigorous, and unnecessarily complex. One person's sacred text is not always another's treasure.

The *Gospel of Thomas* and Zen alike teach that the difference in being *knowers* and not just believers lies not only in what we realize but how we use that understanding in our life. We can stay in our realization of the hidden and the secret, or we can bring ourselves alive like the living Jesus. It is not enough just to see mystery: we must embody it. Some secrets should be exposed to the light.

If a text can't speak to us in our world today, then it is a dead text. The same applies to masters, prophets, messiahs, and teachers. If they are not a living presence in whatever we encounter, then how can they be guides in our lives right now? The *Gospel of Thomas* shows us a Jesus who lives not only in the sayings of *Thomas* but in our very lives.

This eternally accessible and living Jesus speaks in *Thomas*. Its prologue points this out to us right from the beginning.

2

THE DEATHLESS

And he said, "Whoever discovers the meaning of these words won't taste death."

—Gospel of Thomas, saying 1

When you have attained your self-nature, you can free yourself from life-and-death. How will you free yourself from life-and-death when the light of your eyes is falling to the ground? When you have freed yourself from life-and-death, you know where to go. After your four elements have decomposed, where will you go?

—Gateless Gate, case 47

Saying 1, like Majjhima Nikaya 1, announces the bottom line for the *Gospel of Thomas*: "The doors to the deathless are open!" The wisdom of Jesus offers freedom from death, and this is within the grasp of anyone who seeks it. Saying 1 suggests that this freedom is not a matter of finding the one true interpretation of each saying, but the meaning derived from our own experience and wisdom.

When we read *Thomas*, we have to remind ourselves that our true spiritual task is not to memorize or merely learn the meaning given to us by a master; it is to *become* the meaning itself. The sayings of *Thomas*, like koans, are not fixed pieces of information; they are pointers to our direct experience of the universe, reminders, perhaps of what we already know but have forgotten. We can see this in the famous collection of koans called the *Gateless Gate*, in case 6, "Buddha Holds up a Flower":

> Once in ancient times, when the World-Honored One [the Buddha] was at Mount Grdhrakuta, he held up a flower, twirled it, and showed it to the assemblage. At this, they all remained silent. Only the venerable Kashyapa broke into a smile. The World-Honored One said, "I have the eye treasury of the true Dharma, the marvelous mind of nirvana, the true form of no-form, the subtle gate of the Dharma. It does not depend on letters, being specially transmitted outside all teachings. Now I entrust Mahakashyapa with this."

Mahakashyapa didn't need any words to explain that he knew the Buddha's meaning. The master did not tell him what the "marvelous mind of nirvana" actually meant; Mahakashyapa worked it out in his own way, recognizing what had been there all along—his own true nature. The encounter with the Buddha and the flower had directly pointed to the eternal.

The purpose of not revealing profound mystery upfront is to make sure that the religious practitioner works for their meal—the feast of enlightenment, intimately experienced. To say too much to students would make them into thieves, stealing the true meaning from adepts who have already reached realization. This is not the Jesus in the *Gospel of Thomas*, the person who in saying 62 discloses logion to those "who are worthy of mysteries." This Jesus wants us to see and confirm with our own eyes.

So what is it that we come to see and know?

We come to know the deathlessness of the true self. This true self is the inconceivable, beginningless, endless, omniscient, primordial, and aware truth. This is very different from the little ego-self we have built up—something most of us simply do not see. We see only one side of things—the relative, phenomenal side. We are aware only of what we can see with our eyes, not what we cannot. And so we suffer, lost in the wilderness without the knowledge of who we really are. Many of the disciples in the *Gospel of Thomas* are like this.

When we acquire deep wisdom we see that nothing is really separate and that all things are connected. This connectedness is our true nature, which is also the nature of the ultimate. In seeing this intimately, we enter the Kingdom—the eternal rest and cessation of suffering. This true nature is both deathless and unborn.

My Dharma grandfather (my teacher's teacher), Koun Yamada Roshi, used to explain the essential and the relative or conventional sides of life by comparing them to two sides of the hand—together they make one thing. You can't have one side without the other. They're different, but together they are both needed for the whole thing to work.

Or we might think of it with regard to waves on the ocean: every wave is unique and specific, but it is also always just the ocean, never separate from the ocean itself. Every wave does "die," but at the same time it doesn't. There was never anything separate to die because nothing separate was born in the first place. In this way we don't *obtain* immortality, but rather we *are* immortality.

The *Surangama Sutra* tells us that what changes is subject to destruction, whereas the unchanging is beyond birth and death. The form of the wave dies, but the ocean itself never does. Our inherent nature cannot die because it is the inherent nature of the Kingdom.

In case 47 of the *Gateless Gate* Zen Master Dumshuai Congyueh asked his disciples, "How would you free yourself from life and death when the light of your eyes is falling?"—at the very moment of your death. Like Jesus, Congyueh prompts his disciples to make use of every moment as an opportunity for enlightenment, an opportunity to realize the deathless as our very selves.

In the whole of *Thomas*, the living Jesus, like the living Buddha, beats the drum of deathlessness in a world gone blind—and warns us not to let the deathless be lost on us.

3

QUALITIES OF
ENLIGHTENED PEOPLE

Jesus said, "The older person won't hesitate to ask a little seven-day-old child about the place of life, and they'll live, because many who are first will be last, and they'll become one and the same."

—*Gospel of Thomas*, saying 4

A monk asked Zhaozhou, "Does a newborn baby have the sixth consciousness or not?" Zhaozhou said, "Bouncing a ball upon swift waters." The monk also asked Touzi Datong, "What does 'bouncing a ball upon swift waters' mean?" Touzi Datong said, "Thought by thought, the flow never stops."

—*Blue Cliff Record*, case 80

Saying 4 gives a suggestion about the qualities of a teacher and the way in which a person can embody the truth in an authentic manner. As a good teacher himself, Jesus also recognized what the Buddha knew—that "it is hard to meet someone who can explain the truth and harder to meet an enlightened person—but it is hardest to believe in their teaching" because this requires us to experience truth for ourselves.

One way to identify a realized teacher is to pay attention to the way they model enlightened behavior. This holds true for the old man since he is humble enough to ask a small child about the place of life, that is, about the Kingdom, or what some people would call the ground of being.

We would normally expect a child to ask an elder for wisdom, but this old man is wise enough to learn from anything and anyone. He has clearly recognized the child as a source of wisdom because it has not yet formed the conceptual barriers and attachments that adults possess. A child this young does not know anything but the present and is neither male nor female in behavior. As saying 46 reminds us, whoever among you becomes a child will know the Kingdom.

Case 80 of the *Blue Cliff Record*, "Zhaozhou's Newborn Baby," another key koan text, illustrates this. It concerns a monk who asks Master Zhaozhou whether a baby has thoughts and ideas—with the subtext being a question about whether a baby is enlightened because it's just a baby. Not buying into intellectual debate, Zhaozhou cuts to the chase: "Bouncing a ball upon swift waters." Bewildered, the monk asks Touzi Datong, "What does that mean?" Touzi Datong said, "Thought by thought, the flow never stops."

They are describing the baby's moment-to-moment awareness like a ball floating on a swift stream. No attachments, no holding. They are suggesting that, moment to moment, we should drop our preconceptions and react appropriately; that we act from essential nature without weeds clogging up the system. That's enlightenment.

The two teachers are also pointing out that although a newborn baby has consciousness, it hasn't yet bought into superior and inferior or right and wrong as total reality. Like a realized person, it has no attachment to categories, philosophy, or intellection. It has much to teach the adult. Master Zhaozhou is a good example of someone who is open to learning from anyone and anything. He once set out on a pilgrimage vowing that if he met someone wiser than himself he would ask them for instruction—even if they were only seven years old—and if he met someone less wise, he would help them out by giving instruction.

Both Jesus and Zhaozhou recognized that matters of age and gender are not so important, but what matters is how clear a person's insight is. Age is not always a guarantee of wisdom. Both of them reversed the usual order, with the first being last and the last being the first. The old man and the child exchanged places—the two became one and the same, just as they always had been.

As Zen Master Eihei Dogen said in Gyoji Dokan or "Circle of the Way in Continuous Practice" in his Shobogenzo, "it is a wonderful achievement, like a thirsty person finding water." *Thomas* 58 states "congratulations to the person who has toiled and has found life."

In another Zen conversation we have the monk Bai Juyi asking Master Niaoko Daolin, "Just what is the main intention of the Buddha Dharma?" Daolin replied, "To refrain from all evil, to cultivate good, and to purify one's mind." Bai Juyi scoffed, "That's pretty simple, even a child of three knows how to say that!" Daolin replied, "Yes, a three-year-old can say it, but even eighty-year-olds still can't do it." As the *Dhammapada* tells us, this shows that a man is not wise just because his hair's gone gray—he may have many years on him, but he is called "old-in-vain" if he knows the doctrine but not the application or the spirit of it. He is but a student who still has much to learn.

An example of this is found in the *Lotus Sutra* when Shariputra, one of the two chief male disciples of the Buddha, flatly rejects the possibility of a young eight-year-old girl becoming enlightened. After all, she is young and female—conditions that, in that time and place, were regarded as inauspicious. And yet this young girl promptly has an enlightenment experience and proves Shariputra wrong. In this sutra Shariputra is used to illustrate the inappropriate behavior resulting from attachment to one's own state of realization and gender. He is the opposite of the man old in days who will not hesitate to ask a small child about the place of life.

In fact, whatever and whomever we learn from is not important. *That* we learn is the point. Note that Jesus says "many" who are first will become last and vice versa. He does not say *all*. This is another teaching point of this saying—it is difficult to lose our sense of ego-self, and not all of us are up to the task. Matthew 22:14 makes clear that "many shall be called but few shall be chosen." In saying 4 Jesus invites all of us to seek "the place of life" but whether we do or not is entirely up to us. Fortunately everything can be a teacher because everything is emptiness and contains the whole world in itself.

Emptiness is a much misunderstood term but basically it means that since everything is joined, separateness does not ultimately exist. It is dynamic universal connection unlimited by finite substance. In one sense, things are separate, and in an ultimate sense they are not. There is only the interpenetrative truth of emptiness; both wave and ocean exist at the same time.

When separation is dissolved, the eternal appears. Saying 4 confirms the fact that while it is true there are individual teachers and students, at the same time this must be balanced by the wider awareness of the universal equality of emptiness. We must also embody this knowledge; it is not enough just to know the sacred texts and doctrine alone. Our actions and our knowledge must align in our life.

To fully enter the eternal is to know the place where the first and the last are the same. It is "the place of life," the very same place in saying 50 "where the Light came into being" and, according to saying 24, not only the very place the disciples should seek to be, but where Jesus dwells as well.

4

THE MUSTARD SEED
AND THE OAK TREE

The disciples asked Jesus, "Tell us, what can the kingdom of heaven be compared to?" He said to them, "It can be compared to a mustard seed. Though it's the smallest of all the seeds, when it falls on tilled soil it makes a plant so large that it shelters the birds of heaven."

—*Gospel of Thomas*, saying 20

A monk asked Zhaozhou, "What is the meaning of the ancestor's coming from the West?" Zhaozhou said, "The oak tree there in the garden."

—*Book of Equanimity*, case 47

In saying 20 the disciples ask what the Kingdom of heaven is like—in many koans an unrealized person, usually a monk, will ask a master a very similar question. In a certain sense, such questions are about the nature of the essential self.

Like Jesus, the Buddha and other enlightened people would sometimes answer these kinds of questions using similes such as it is like "the plum tree in spring," "the flag on the pole blown in the wind," "one flower preaching the boundless spring," or "one drop of water revealing the waters of the great ocean." In case 47 of the *Book of Equanimity*, a collection of koans compiled in the thirteenth century, a monk asked Master Zhaozhou, "What is the meaning of the ancestor's coming from the West?" Zhaozhou said, "The oak tree there in the garden." The question refers to Bodhidharma, the first ancestor of Zen who brought Zen to China. So in a nutshell the monk is asking what the essence of Zen Buddhism is or "What's the bottom line for all of this?"

How can something as plain as an old oak tree be the great truth? In an important way, we might also ask, why not? The oak tree is the Kingdom, too. It too is emptiness, complete in itself, not separate from anything or anyone. It fully occupies its roots, branches, and leaves. I'm not sure many human beings can truly say they fully occupy their own skin.

Something as ordinary and small as a seed carries the DNA of the Kingdom and can grow exponentially if it is properly attended to. To recognize the Kingdom within ourselves is to grow tall and to be a refuge and a shelter for ourselves and others. The Buddha noted that unfortunately most of us look for refuge in all sorts of places while ignoring our essential self. Yet true rest can come only through recognition of the true and unitive nature of the universe. "That is the safe refuge, the best refuge," the Buddha said. "Having gone to that refuge, a person is delivered from all pain." Knowing the Kingdom is to fully rest in our own skin.

While we may not initially feel that we can become like the living Jesus, we mustn't think that even a small glimpse of wisdom will not come to fruition in the here and now. Even a small thing such as a mustard seed can help us awaken. This is what a young mother whose child died realized in "Kisa Gotami and the Parable of the Mustard Seed."

In this traditional Buddhist story, a young woman named Kisa Gotami is engulfed by grief when her child dies, so much so that she wanders from house to house with her dead child in her arms asking for help. Feeling compassion for her, one of her neighbors suggests that she go to the Buddha and ask him for help. So when the Buddha was teaching nearby, she went to him and asked for a remedy for the death of her child. The Buddha replied, "I do have medicine for your child, but first I require some mustard seeds taken from a house where no one has died."

Relieved, she went back to her village and began asking her neighbors for mustard seeds. Having placed the dead child on her hip, she searched the entire city, but to her dismay, she could not find a home that had not suffered the loss of a family member. There was not a single family free from impermanence. She could not collect a single mustard seed without also collecting what is universal—death. While undoubtedly Kisa Gotami continued to grieve, the wisdom lesson of impermanence became clear. Clearly, this is a parable of growth since spiritual insight grew from the mustard seed.

While mustard can grow without any human effort, it is also like wisdom in that it expands in ground that is properly prepared. The three elements of this parable are the three elements of a viable and true spiritual path. Knowledge of the Kingdom (1) is attained through skilled effort; (2) it results in an expanded awareness; and (3) just as a mustard seed results in a large branch or refuge when it is placed in tilled soil, so too does knowledge of the Kingdom grow within a mind that is already predisposed toward realization.

The example of the large branch or plant in *Thomas* carries similar lessons to the lotus flower. In Buddhism the lotus is one of the best recognized motifs. Its roots extend into the mud, the stem grows up through the water, and the flower blossoms above the surface. The mud is a metaphor for the dust and grit of daily life, the water represents experience, and the breakthrough into the sunlight represents the light of wisdom.

The lesson of saying 20 is that, just as a lotus uses the murky soil to germinate and through the strength of its own stem comes to fruition in the sunshine, so too can we use insight to choose the right path and transform negative tendencies into positive ones. This is rebirth in a figurative and a literal sense. A Zen meal *gatha* (short verse) says, "May we live in this world of emptiness, like the lotus in muddy water." The *Thomas* version might be "May we exist in the Kingdom with wisdom, like the tree that grows from a mustard seed."

5

RELIANCE

The disciples said to Jesus, "We know that you will leave us. Who will be great among us then?" Jesus told them, "When you find yourselves at that point, go to James the Just. All that concerns heaven and earth is his domain."

—*Gospel of Thomas*, saying 12

I reveal to all beings a device to educate them, albeit I do not really become extinct at the time, and in this very place continue preaching the law. But men of confused minds, in their delusion, do not see me standing there.

—*Lotus Sutra*, chapter 15

Saying 12 concerns the worries and fears that Jesus's disciples have about continuing their spiritual development in the absence of their teacher. It appears that their fears have momentarily overwhelmed their confidence in their own spiritual power. In wisdom traditions generally, authority ultimately rests on the individual, who must live and embody the teachings in their own fully realized way. This can sometimes be overwhelming.

Jesus suggests that "when you find yourselves at that point" where you lack direction or succumb to doubt because he has died, seek out

James the Just. Like Jesus, toward the end of his life the Buddha was approached by some of his followers who felt anxious about who would lead the community. Ananda, the Buddha's cousin, felt extremely upset. How would their spirituality continue to develop without an incarnated teacher? This is no doubt the kind of existential angst felt by the disciples when they said to Jesus, "We know that you will leave us. Who will be great among us then?"

The Buddha addressed the same concern and reminded his followers that although his physical body would no longer be here, his teaching body, the *dharmakaya*, would always be with his disciples. In the *Awakening of Faith*, a key text that summarizes the essentials of Mahayana Buddhism, this dharmakaya is described as the eternal, the blessed, the self-regulating, the pure, the tranquil, the immutable, and the free. It is ultimate reality, the universal ground of being out of which all things arise.

As the primary truth, D. T. Suzuki once described it as the uncreated, ultimate cause of the universe in which all existences find their essential order and significance. This all-pervading nature is suggested by the Buddha's own statement upon reaching enlightenment: "I was, am, and will be enlightened instantaneously with the universe."

The law of origin, as taught by the Nichiren sect of Buddhism, declares that Shakyamuni has continually taught people throughout the universe since the infinite past. The Cosmic Buddha has existed everywhere in the universe since its beginning. In the *Lotus Sutra*, this eternal Buddha reassures his followers saying, "I always stay here and expound the Law." The individual Gotama passed away, but not the Cosmic Buddha, even though—the sutra tells us—in their delusion, most people can't perceive him.

A realized person knows this truth—that the ultimate, which is wisdom itself, never goes away. It is always here. This is what Jesus wants his disciples to recognize and is why he stresses that wherever they are they have access to the ultimate. This is also why he advised them, "when you find yourselves at that point (of doubt about the Kingdom and the teaching), go to James the Just: All that concerns heaven and earth is his domain."

One way we can regard this statement is to take "James the Just" as a metaphor for a wisdom tradition or an enlightened teacher who embodies that wisdom. On one hand, it is not profitable to become the student of an unwise teacher. In James 3:1 we find a warning about the responsibility of teaching: "Not many of you should become teachers . . . for you know that we who teach will be judged with greater strictness." Thankfully, Jesus has directed the disciples to one who is just and wise.

On the other hand, we can also remind ourselves James the Just is not just James the Just. Like all of us, he is also the living Jesus, the Kingdom itself. This is why "all that concerns heaven and earth is his domain" because the cosmic Christ, he who "fills the universe in all its parts" (Ephesians 1:23), has filled James, the disciples, the teachings, and all of heaven and earth.

We can hear the lesson of saying 12 for Jesus's disciples is that to go to James the Just is not only to learn from an enlightened master but to fully connect with the Kingdom ourselves. This can be done whether the incarnated Jesus is alive or not and whether James the Just is alive or not. This deeper meaning must be seen for the disciples to eliminate their sense of being rudderless and to recognize their own authority in arousing the one mind. No one is ever alone or cut off from the eternal, and in times when we feel that this is so, we can remind ourselves that the Kingdom is in this very place, standing right here.

6

THE FORM OF PURITY

If you fast, you will be at fault. If you pray, you will be wrong.
If you give to charity, you will corrupt your mind. When you
go into any land and walk through the countryside, if they
welcome you, eat whatever they offer you. You can heal their
sick. It is not what goes into your mouth that defiles you, it is
what comes out of your mouth that defiles you.

—*Gospel of Thomas*, saying 14

Whenever Master Baizhang Huaihai delivered a sermon, an
old man was always there listening with the monks. When
they left, he left, too. One day, however, he remained behind.
The master asked him, "What man are you, standing in front
of me?" The man replied, "Indeed, I am not a man. In the past,
in the time of Kashyapa Buddha, I lived on this mountain as a
Zen priest. On one occasion a monk asked me, 'Does a perfectly
enlightened person fall under the law of cause and effect or
not?' I answered, 'He does not.' Because of this answer, I fell
into the state of a fox for 500 lives. Now, I beg you, master,
please say something and release me from the body of a fox."
Then he asked, "Does a perfectly enlightened person fall under
the law of cause and effect or not?" The master answered, "The
law of cause and effect cannot be obscured."

—*Gateless Gate*, case 2

Saying 14 hints at the role of rites and piety in religious life, as well as attachments to intellectual and demonstrative forms of purity. It points the truth seeker in the direction of heartfelt and properly understood right action that arises from a clear understanding of the nature and purpose of religious expression—beyond attachment to mere outward form.

Such outward forms of religion are not automatically a problem in and of themselves, but without a wider framework they can be. If the only thing necessary to follow the Way is to give some sort of outward sign, then piety would be just a matter of decoration rather than the development and nurturing of our universal nature. It would also mean that certain people would be locked out of the system if they were unable to manifest whatever sign is supposed to indicate purity. This seems out of sync with the universal and compassionate wisdom of the living Jesus.

It would be easy to think that in saying 14 Jesus is rejecting fasting, praying, and giving to charity outright. If we step back and look at the wider picture, we can see that what he is saying is that it is your inner state of consciousness and understanding that should be the most important. Only that kind of inner religious development is truly worthwhile, and without it, outer demonstrations of a religious nature are meaningless.

The *Awakening of Faith* tells us that if we can move beyond the attachment and the desire to cling to distinctions, then we can see that *pure* and *impure* are just relative conditions. This is not saying that they are unimportant but that in buying into them as a finite totality, we become trapped within them.

In the *Platform Sutra* Daijian Huineng, the sixth ancestor of Zen, tells us that the focus of Zen is not upon fostering purity or suppressing impurity. Our nature is intrinsically pure, he says, and if we abandon attachment to our conceptual boxes, then what's left over is the purity of our true self. If we direct our mind to dwell upon purity, we are only creating another delusion: the delusion of purity.

He goes further and says that some people go so far as to invent the "form of purity" and then treat it as a problem to solve. By hanging on to these forms (such as bowing and chanting) they get hung up on them. They become obsessed with purity. What he is saying, then, is that by entering the Kingdom and returning to our original nature, purity arises by itself. This is an entirely natural process, but if we cling to purity, then this does not give our nature the chance to shine. We just get caught up in categories, judgment, and outward forms of piety. We obscure the true self.

In the famous fox koan, case 2 of the *Gateless Gate*, Master Baizhang Huaihai spoke to an old man who had always been lingering around the monastery. The old man related that he had once been a Zen priest. When he had taught that a perfectly enlightened person is outside of the law of cause and effect, the priest had been reborn as a fox for 500 lives. In Japanese folklore foxes are figures of mischief and magic, so this is, in one sense, the result of wrongdoing. Clearly he had done something wrong to warrant this. He begged the master to sort this out for him by answering one question, "Does a perfectly enlightened person fall under the law of cause and effect or not?" The master answered, "The law of cause and effect cannot be obscured."

What is going on here? Well, it's the classic problem of sticking to one position only. The former priest was entirely correct in saying that an enlightened man is not affected by karma. In emptiness there is no karma and no one to cause it. If everything is one, who's there to affect? There's no separate person for karma to attach to. Karma has no jurisdiction in emptiness. While this is true, if it is taken to the extreme—as the only truth—it can result in something like the Buji Zen of medieval Japan, in which people mistakenly excused the need to follow moral and ethical precepts, to put effort into learning the doctrines and sutras of Buddhism, or even to develop their own capabilities in order to see true reality. They thought that because they were already children of the Kingdom (purely by virtue of having been born human) they never had to seek out the truth. Everything they did was perfectly acceptable no matter how unethical, because it's "all buddha nature anyway." Since everything is the eternal, any action was acceptable. This kind of thinking was nihilistic, conceptually rigid, unethical, and impractical.

The priest is not as bad as this, but he still gave only half the story. Both halves are always essential. This means that while we are emptiness itself, we still have individual bodies and actions to affect. These two facts occur at the same time. We cannot ever escape our karma because while everything is emptiness it is also form (the quality of solidity, separateness, and definition). In terms of Jesus and saying 14, the lesson here is that Jesus is not dismissing praying, fasting, and giving outright just because everything is one in the Kingdom. It's putting them in their proper context that is important.

We do this by abandoning attachment to two notions—that certain acts are either pure in and of themselves or that we become pure just by doing them. If we are attached to these ideas, then fasting, praying, giving to charity, and observing dietary rules are not necessarily connected to any particular state of mind because they can bypass the need for inner development and insight. They can be done merely as empty actions without any context or conscious connection to truth seeking.

Seen in this light, giving to charity would be an ego-driven event without a solid ethical base. As the *Diamond Sutra* reminds us, when we give away things we should give with selfless kindness. This means that we should remind ourselves that there is essentially no distinction between our own self and the selfhood of others. It's not skillful to get hung up on the "I" who is giving to "them"—that creates a false separation.

Thus Jesus warns the disciples that, in their current state of attachment to the letter and not the spirit, if they give to charity, they will corrupt their mind. If they pray merely for good fortune or because they are supposed to, then this is not the right manner in which to pray because our whole life should be a prayer, and the actual act of putting our hands together is the natural outflow of this state of being. The same can be said for fasting and all other such things.

The Buddha himself learned the foolishness of fasting for the wrong reason and to the wrong degree. As with many renunciants of his time, he tried achieving purification through rigorous self-mortification. He hoped to set free his mind from the shackles of his body. He fasted in an extreme manner and in time became emaciated and weak. Eventually he realized that despite his efforts, his attachments still remained. Having realized that extreme asceticism only robs us of energy, he renounced severe self-discipline. The Buddha found that fasting from delusion was more productive.

Jesus himself did not reject the world but overcame it. This is what he wants for his followers, too, but it is they who must take steps to cut their attachments to worldly or outward measurements of religious truth. Without doing this, they cannot find the Kingdom. If they do not put their heart and soul into making each day the Sabbath instead of merely making the appropriate gestures and actions, then no manner of fasting will bring the wisdom of the living Jesus.

Jesus challenges his followers to be flexible and to ride the to and fro of skillful means. So if they are welcomed and offered food, then rather than fretting about breaking the precept of fasting, they should receive the food in the manner in which it was offered.

The Buddha, too, gave this advice to his monastic followers who were sometimes given meat when on alms rounds. Keep the precept of not killing, he said, but should someone kill an animal (whether especially for you or otherwise) and place its meat in your begging bowl, accept it in the manner in which it was given, with a spirit of generosity. In this way both the letter and the spirit are taken care of.

Essentially, then, it comes down to this: Jesus is not going to do such things as praying and fasting for their own sake, especially when he has not done anything that warrants penitent expression. Instead, he says, when we have married the outer and the inner and have become whole, then and only then can we move beyond the extremes of "I must" and "I needn't."

When we have met the living one within ourselves, only then do we overcome our views about pious performances. Then we can express a variety of religious expressions at will and at appropriate times without being torn between "should I?" and "should I not?" This is the middle way beyond the two extremes. The Anguttara Nikaya describes this state, saying that for a person who is in full possession of virtue, there is no need for the purposeful thought, "May freedom from remorse arise in me, may joy arise in me, and may rapture arise in me." These mind states happen naturally when we have fully realized essential nature.

In this enlightened state a person is not constrained by fixed dualities. This does not mean that such a person is therefore immoral. Rather, such a person has reached a stage where they have totally incorporated their religion and it has stopped being an intellectual idea. They are no longer giving to charity because they have been told to, for example, but because they have become charity itself. Saying 14 suggests to us that this is the stage we must reach if we are to open the doors to the deathless.

7

Listen and See!

Jesus [said], "The Father's kingdom can be compared to a woman who took a little yeast and [hid] it in flour. She made it into large loaves of bread. Anyone who has ears to hear should hear!"

—*Gospel of Thomas*, saying 96

Therefore it is said: The supreme one way can't be transmitted even by the thousand holy ones. Practitioners who labor for forms are like monkeys trying to grasp reflections. Just tell me, if it can't be transmitted, why are there so many entangling koans? Those who have an eye to see, let them see!

—*Blue Cliff Record*, case 12

Saying 96 points out that what is not apparent to the eye can be the cause of awakening. The concealed yeast can be heard as a metaphor for essential nature, that which cannot be conceptualized but can be experienced. Just as the yeast permeates the whole loaf, so too does the uncreated eternal pervade the entire universe.

Thomas's frequent emphasis upon effort to produce a good result is evident in the fact that bread has to be kneaded and left to rest before it can be cooked and raised. Thus, the Kingdom is not just a woman but a woman who takes action—and under the right conditions, a little seed and a little leaven produce a huge result. The message for human consciousness is the same.

It might seem odd that the woman concealed the yeast, but again, this is symbolic of the fact that its functioning, like spiritual growth, may not be fully apparent from the outside. The Buddha pointed this out in an analogy in the Samyutta Nikaya about a carpenter and his cutting tool.

> To the mason or his apprentice, the marks of the fingers and the mark of the hand become apparent on the handle of the adze. Yet he does not know, "This much of the handle has worn down today, or tomorrow it is this much," but he knows that the handle has got wasted. In the same manner to the monk dwelling yoked to the development of the mind, even if knowledge does not arise, "Today this much of the defilements have been destroyed and tomorrow it is this much," he knows that they have been destroyed.

We must not get discouraged if we don't see big changes. Just because we don't become enlightened overnight or even after years is still no reason to give up. Bit by bit we can grow into fully embodying the Kingdom. From small things big things grow.

Ignatius of Loyola converted Francis Xavier by quoting a verse of scripture, and the sixth ancestor of Zen, Daijian Huineng, attained realization upon hearing a fragment of the *Diamond Sutra*. The Kingdom is already within us—this is why we can be transformed through simple causation. If we foster it, the Kingdom can permeate our entire life.

In Mahayana Buddhism one term for the Kingdom within is the *tathagatagarbha*, the indwelling Buddha essence. The exact meaning of the expression is "containing a buddha," referring to the fact that all of us have a buddha within us in seed or embryo form. Since sentient beings have a buddha core or essential inner nature, we are the "wombs" of the Tathagata. When we have clear sight of this it is called "giving birth to a buddha."

Like the yeast concealed in bread, it has traditionally been compared to such things as honey protected by bees, kernels enclosed by their husks, the pit inside a mango, hidden treasure beneath the house, or a sprout in the seed becoming a huge tree. The *Song of Enlightenment*, a poem much favored by Zen, laments the fact that people do not recognize this jewel, our essential nature, within: it operates our sight, hearing, smell, taste, sensation, awareness, and yet we do not see it. It is consciousness of this that the disciples need to foster, according to saying 96.

The idea of this hidden essential nature is reinforced in saying 113 when the disciples are again using only their physical sight to look for the Kingdom. They ask Jesus, "When will the Kingdom come?" He replies, "It won't come by looking for it. They won't say, 'Look over here!' or 'Look over there!' Rather, the Father's kingdom is already spread out over the earth, and people don't see it."

No wonder Master Dongshan Shouchou in case 12 of the *Blue Cliff Record* shouted to his students, "Those who have an eye to see, let them see!" He and Jesus could no doubt shout this together. In this case his disciples were getting caught up in concepts and were wondering how awakening could be transmitted when essential nature is beyond concepts. Master Dongshan acknowledged the trickiness in meshing the essential and the phenomenal.

"Yes, you're right," he said, "the supreme one way can't be transmitted even by the thousand holy ones. Practitioners who labor for forms are like monkeys trying to grasp reflections. Just tell me, if it can't be transmitted, why are there so many entangling koans? Those who have an eye to see, let them see!" In other words, just because something is indescribable doesn't mean it can't be experienced, and koans, like sayings, can help us do this. Clear sight of this is a must for realization. We can do this right here, right now.

We must not mistake the Kingdom for a future event when it is a state of transformed consciousness, a nondual awareness invisible to the eye. We cannot pin this down to an exact spot or measure it with a yardstick—but it can be cultivated in the present and it does change us. It occurs not so much in our lives but in how we relate to our lives. It goes deeper than that, however.

As I said before, we cannot capture the ultimate in conceptualizations, philosophy, or intellection. Moreover, if the Kingdom is both inside and outside, it is not a separate thing to see, as if somehow we could point to a particular object and say, "That's it!" The Way is complete in itself. It is not spatially or temporally separate from the disciples. It is everywhere here and now.

If the disciples are to take anything away from their question-and-answer session, they must fully realize and implement the five advantages of listening to the Word that are listed in the Anguttara Nikaya: we hear things not previously heard, clarify things previously heard, dispel doubts, straighten our views, and calm our heart. The doors to the deathless are open for those who would hear.

As Jesus told us: "The Father's kingdom can be compared to a woman." She is representative of all of us because all of us have the very same nature as she. This gives us a good reason to follow the injunction of sayings 8 and 96: "Anyone here with two good ears had better listen!" Both sayings send forth the missive that the doors of the immortal are open, so let those who can hear respond with faith. The *Dhammapada* reminds us that the unlistening man matures like an ox: his muscles develop but his discernment doesn't.

The choice is clear.

8

SEEKING AND FINDING

Jesus said, "Whoever seeks shouldn't stop until they find. When they find, they'll be disturbed. When they're disturbed, they'll be [. . .] amazed, and reign over the All."

—*Gospel of Thomas*, saying 2

Immediately after birth the Buddha stood firmly on his feet, and having taken seven strides to the north, uttered in a fearless voice the lion's roar: "Above heaven and below heaven, I alone am the World-Honored One."

—Digha Nikaya 14

Here, the Jesus of *Thomas* outlines a developmental process on the path to realization that can be successful only through conscious, active, and individual effort. The stages of this process are seeking and finding, finding and being disturbed, being disturbed and ruling, ruling and resting. A person who follows these steps will come to live a completely transformed life and acquire a new way of understanding the self and the ultimate.

Saying 2 makes a promise to us: we have an inherent nature that motivates us to look for enlightenment. It suggests that at any one time there is a feedback loop occurring—our true nature is simultaneously

the basis and the goal. It is our true self that makes us seek enlightenment, and it is seeking that makes us realize we have it. We can't do
anything else since it is who and what we are.

In case 16 of the *Blue Cliff Record*, "Jingqing Daofu and Picking
and Pecking," a monk asked Master Daofu, "I, your student, am picking
from inside the shell. I beg you, master, please peck from outside." Daofu
said, "But will you be alive or not?" The monk said, "If I were not alive,
people would all laugh." Daofu said, "You fool in the weeds!"

Whenever you see the words *weeds* or *grass* in Zen it refers to wading
through the mud of thoughts. So this reply from Master Daofu is Zen-
speak for the fact that the monk is caught up in his own head. To add to
this, if Daofu helped the monk too much he'd be giving him the answer.
He would not be alive or dead but somewhere in between.

What Daofu is trying to get across is the fact that it does not
matter about inside and outside, life and death; what matters is the
pecking itself—the seeking itself. Just that in itself is everything. To
realize this is to break out of our shell of ignorance. As saying 94 of
Thomas says: "Whoever looks will find; whoever knocks from inside,
it will open to them."

It is because we do not seek the truth or recognize our true nature
that we are uneasy and discontent in the world. To seek until we find
is an attempt to restore ourselves to our original wholeness. When we
see the whole picture, we also see that there is an inevitability to finding and to being let into the Kingdom. After all, how can we not find
something that is already here, and how can we not be let in when we
are already "inside." It is not a matter of inventing something new; it
is a matter of opening our eyes to what has always been here. If this
were a koan, it might be called "Nothing lost, nothing locked." There
was never anything lost to find and no locked doors in front of it in
the first place.

So no matter how much we may doubt ourselves, the first stage of
the process—seeking and finding—is completely natural to all spiritual

paths. It is the finding and being disturbed stage that might catch many people by surprise because we would normally think that when we find the truth, peace and rest would automatically result.

But this is too easy and glib for a gospel that teaches about the secret and deep meaning of wisdom. As the old saying suggests—something that looks too good to be true is probably too good to be true. So the fact that the road is portrayed as multifaceted and the path steep and discomforting is testament to the fact that the *Gospel of Thomas* is honest and upfront with the spiritual traveler.

The road to realization is hard work. It requires self-reflection, a high degree of commitment, and an ability to be honest about our own short-comings. Unsurprisingly, this truth is not met with enthusiasm by all spiritual seekers. A common pattern in some Zen centers in the West is that people come with all sorts of unrealistic notions about Zen, so that when they see that it takes time and effort they leave.

Not only does saying 2 concern the path but also the fruits of it. It states that finding the essential equates with being troubled or dismayed. This is why, in saying 84 of *Thomas*, Jesus says to the disciples, "When you see your likeness, you rejoice. But when you see your images that came into being before you did—which don't die, and aren't revealed—how much you'll have to bear!" In other words, will they be able to handle it when they realize their essential self?

Some translations use the phrase "will you be able to stand it?" Ordinarily we would expect a sense of lightness at seeing our true self, and this does of course happen. At the same time, this is no stock-standard *aha!* moment. Now that we have awakened to the deathless there is also a heightened awareness of responsibility.

We can no longer deny what we know and believe in superficialities anymore. We can't go back and cover our eyes. We must work on our initial glimpse of wisdom and put down whatever is holding us back no matter how beloved it may be. This "burden" means that we realize new life requires death after death, and this is not comfortable even when metaphorical. While the secrets of the living Jesus deliver life, we must completely die first for resurrection and true living to occur.

Yet in saying 2, Jesus reassures us that this troubling loss of self and the recognition that all our concepts, constructs, and belief systems simply don't do the universe justice will be balanced by a sense of astonishment and wonder. We will marvel at what we now see and know. This is the experience of *metanoia*, the entire transformation of who and what we are. We realize how amazing our true identity is and the level to which we are now empowered. This childlike wonder is what enables us to "reign over the All."

To be clear, this reigning over totality shouldn't be interpreted in terms of domination and control. Knowing the secrets of the living Jesus does not mean that we end up lords over everything and everyone since, as the *Dhammapada* points out, conquering ourselves is better than conquering all other people: "If one man conquers in battle a thousand times thousand men, and if another conquers himself, he is the greatest of conquerors." It is only this kind of "reigning" that delivers real freedom.

Pointing out the way in order to be in a position of power over others is too ordinary a concern for the *Gospel of Thomas*. If occupying a position of power or worldly authority were considered the central (and deeper) meaning of this saying, it would indicate that we have seen only the phenomenal side of reality and not the essential as well. It would be shortsighted because it suggests a view that still separates self and other. Anyone can hold this view; it requires no wisdom at all.

To achieve the deathless something more than this worldly kind of ruling is needed for rest and peace to occur. Thus it is traditionally believed in Buddhism that better than sovereignty over the earth, better than going to heaven, better than lordship over all worlds, is the reward of the first step on the Way. When the Buddha was born, a learned holy man, Kaundinya, was called upon to predict his future. He predicted that the young boy had an interesting choice ahead of him—either he was to be a universal ruler or he would renounce the world and become a supreme religious leader. Siddhartha Gotama eventually chose the latter. He had recognized that until we find our essential nature we cannot be in a true winning position.

The deeper meaning of reigning over totality, then, is to dissolve the gap between the separate self and everything else. According to one of the many legends built around the Buddha's birth, it is said that when he was born he walked seven steps in each direction and pointed to the heavens with one hand and to the earth with the other. He said, "Above heaven and below heaven, I alone am the World-Honored One."

At first glance this appears a hugely egotistical statement, but as with saying 2 we mustn't mistake the surface meaning for the deeper one. This "I" is not just the individual self of the Buddha alone. It is not the "I" of the ego-self but the true self—the ultimate. This "I" is everything and everyone. The Buddha had stepped out of his bounded, separate self into the whole. In essence he had realized that "I alone" meant that altogether everything is nothing but ourselves; there is nothing outside of us. This is "self as Buddha, everything as Buddha" or "one is all, all is one."

In this way we reign from a position of total unity and equality because we can truly say to ourselves that "above heaven and below heaven" the whole universe is myself right here, right now. This is vastly more than any worldly position of power could ever deliver. And in saying 2, Jesus suggests that only when we see this can we find true rest and repose.

This repose is knowledge of the true nature of reality, the manifestation of perfect rest or what is also known in Theravada Buddhism as "rest of the blessed." Since this is something we can do in the present, we don't have to wait until death for peace in this world. The repose of wisdom is said to be, among other things, quiet and at rest, illuminating, peaceful, and bliss producing.

So while a person might experience the rewards of awakening, they must always continue seeking and finding. Our sense of a separate self often resists any attempt to surrender it before wisdom. Sometimes we may backslide and have to seek again until we find. Only then we will rest in the essential once more.

Entering the Kingdom—entering enlightenment—is a *process* with an open end, rather than a set of steps that result in a one-off static state.

Only when we realize this will true repose become an authentic and righteous signpost that we can truly live by.

9

KNOW YOURSELF

If those who guide you say: Look, the Kingdom is in the sky, then the birds are closer than you. If they say: Look, it is in the sea, then the fish already know it. The Kingdom is inside you, and it is outside you. When you know yourself, then you will be known, and you will know that you are the child of the Living Father; but if you do not know yourself, you will live in vain and you will be vanity.

—*Gospel of Thomas*, saying 3

When a fish moves, the water is muddied; when a bird flies, feathers drop.

—*Blue Cliff Record*, case 29

Saying 3 contains a warning from Jesus to be cautious about immediately accepting whatever a teacher-guide says about the Kingdom. This is a continuing theme throughout *Thomas*: teachers give us guidance, but in the end we must work out the true meaning of the Kingdom for ourselves through wisdom and insight.

We must truly see what is going on because it is only when we see our enslavement to our own ego and self-based concepts that we can also see the Kingdom. The vanity mentioned in this saying is an illusion based on ultimate individuality, that is, the misperception that sees the separate self (and its intellectual capacities) as the central decider of what's true. Anyone who enshrines this self-system makes it difficult to enter the Kingdom—and those who are too self-invested find it difficult to change.

It is understandable, then, that some translations have not used the word *vanity* but *poverty* to describe a state that embodies a lack of understanding. This is not poverty in a positive sense as in poor of ego, but poor in wisdom, poor in the truth, and poor in accepting alternate ways of being.

Jesus's disciples appear to be rich in concepts that prevent them from breaking out of established doctrine and of their preconceived ideas of where the Kingdom is. They have probably heard others talk of the Kingdom as located in a specific time and space. They are troubled because they're struggling with certain cherished concepts, but they don't recognize that they could actually be on the verge of finding wisdom if they could only drop those concepts.

And thus Jesus tells it to them straight and suggests that even birds and fish, who embody their own nature freely, have grasped their fullness in the light. Fish and birds entertain no idea that they are fish and birds, nor do they know anything other than where and what they are. With their limited capacities, they totally occupy their life positions with all their hearts and minds. They live fully in their world, which is the Kingdom itself.

This Kingdom is the very ground of being on which we stand. This is why when Zen Master Dasui Fazhen was asked, "Buddha's truth is everywhere, so where do you teach students to plant their feet?" he answered, "When a fish moves, the water is muddied; when a bird flies, feathers drop." Both the fish and the bird are just doing their thing—and so is everything and everyone else.

As the Buddha's saying "I alone am the World-Honored One" portrays, there is no separation between the essential and the phenomenal.

This means that outside of this moment there is nothing else, so everything is totally what it is at that time. Every moment is the point at which the one and the many, distinction and sameness, stand in totality.

Zen Master Eihei Dogen was especially good at expressing the absolute present—and used imagery similar to that used by the Jesus of *Thomas*. In *Actualizing the Fundamental Point*, Dogen wrote that every creature covers the ground it stands on, no more, no less. It never falls short of completeness. Everything is absolutely consummate in its own right. As Dogen coined it elsewhere, everything is in its own "being-time." Accordingly, the disciples are not as wise as the fish and the bird because they do not recognize their own being-time. Dogen points out what they could've learned from the two animals: "A fish swims in the ocean, and no matter how far it swims there is no end to the water. A bird flies in the sky, and no matter how far it flies there is no end to the air. Thus, each of them totally covers its full range, and each of them totally experiences its realm."

They know their truth position and live it fully. So on one level saying 2 is comparing the limited thinking and discerning abilities of the disciples to that of mere animals because they think only in temporal, spatial terms. But on a deeper level it is a concrete teaching point about knowing the nature of reality.

So unlike fish and birds, the disciples do not fully occupy their Dharma position (their truth position) since their experience of life is to wish to be somewhere else where supposedly the Kingdom of Heaven is. They do not live in the eternal now with eternally living Jesus but in some dead notion of the future in some other place.

Their Kingdom is not the water because that's the eternal now for fish. Rather, it is talking with Jesus then, at the very moment he was teaching them. At that precise point, in receiving the teachings, the Kingdom presented itself. Realization (entering and living in the Kingdom) is always within this very moment. That was their Dharma position and they missed it because they did not know their own true nature. If they did, they would also know the nature of the Kingdom that is indivisible from their own nature. It is only in this way that we break through self-isolation and become known to the eternal. It knows us and we know it because "I alone am the World-Honored One." Or, as saying 3 puts it, "When you know yourselves, then you will be known, and you will know that you are the child of the Living Father."

As Zen Master Linji Yixuan, founder of the Linji School of Zen, once stated, if you turn your light within yourself, you will come to know that your own mind and those of the buddhas and ancestors are not different. Or we might hear this as, "you will know that you and Jesus are one." You will know your true self and your true potential just as the wave naturally derives its power and very being from the swell of the ocean.

Inside and outside (in an essential sense) are the same, so to know one is to know the other. The living Father does not have size or spatial dimensions, so "inside" and "outside" are mere conceptual traps. To say the Kingdom is only inside is to limit the limitless to our own inner self, and the world could easily be seen as a threatening "other" that must be subdued or ignored. Conversely, if we were to limit the Kingdom to whatever is outside us, then this could lead to an unhealthy self-denial of needs and personal experience. Moreover, since the Kingdom is also within and beyond time and space, linear descriptors such as past and future do not apply either.

And yet so long as we do not know ourselves, we will live in vain because we'll be living a life of separation between us and the Kingdom; between subject and object; between us and Jesus; between us and the past, present, and future. We will be the ego-based and false center of the world when in fact there is no center. It is all one.

This is the warning—and the deep wisdom—that the living Jesus gives to us.

10

Seen and Unseen

Jesus said, "Recognize what is in your sight, and that which is hidden from you will become plain to you. For there is nothing hidden which will not become manifest."

—*Gospel of Thomas*, saying 5

As always, the Venerable Shakyamuni and you walk, stand, sit, and lie down together. He talks and visits with you without the two of you ever being separated even for an instant. If in this lifetime you do not lay eyes on this venerable one, then you will all be thoroughly undutiful beings.

—*Record of Transmitting the Light*, case 2

Saying 5, like Anguttara Nikaya 8:1, makes it clear that "a wise person knows what he ought to know and sees what he ought to see." Jesus tells us we must recognize all of reality, both seen and unseen, because once we do, then by ourselves we thoroughly know and see, face to face, this very universe.

Jesus emphasizes development of spiritual sight because ignorance causes separation of the self and the eternal. Spiritual blindness causes pain and is described in Buddhism as a flood, a yoke, a fetter, an obsession, and the cause of wrong view. Accordingly, recognition of the true nature of reality is the foundation for right understanding, which is the understanding of ourselves as we really are. This is what Jesus is trying to engender in his disciples—the recognition that we should not be tied to mere appearances and forms, but transformed through renewing our minds (Romans 12:2). What we see is not always what is there; we must go deeper to see the living wisdom that is our birthright.

Unfortunately a shortage of spiritual skills has left the disciples spiritually blind and unable to make good choices about what methods to use rather than their usual ones. They are naive in the sense that they expect enlightenment to be describable in words. They look to Jesus for answers but he will have none of this. Instead, he sidesteps their questions and points to the heart of the matter—seek and see or remain blind forever. Unless they examine the present moment, blindness will be their fate.

The disciples seem to think that something other than the world in front of them is the living one and that below the surface the "real" Jesus can be found. Again, Jesus cuts through the concepts and thoughts with a pointed answer—you must remove the blinkers on your eyes. Never mind the inner and outer, the flesh and the spirit, the hidden purity and the outward appearance. Just drop it all. Don't even engage with it.

When a young child plays with abandon, she doesn't get caught up in thinking about quality of the material, the price tag, or what play "really" looks like. She simply picks up and puts down objects at will according to the situation. So when Jesus states that his followers must become precisely like this, he points to the state of unencumbered enlightenment that recognizes the true unitive state of emptiness.

Since the nature of the ultimate and our individual nature are the same and indivisible, to see one thing is to see all. The Buddha said, "He who sees Dharma [truth/reality], sees me; he who sees me, sees Dharma" and Jesus said, "I and my Father are one." To see Jesus is to see the truth, and to see the truth is to see oneself. This is the knowledge that we, too, are the cosmic body of Christ.

BUSINESS REPLY MAIL

FIRST-CLASS MAIL   PERMIT NO. 1100   SOMERVILLE, MA

POSTAGE WILL BE PAID BY ADDRESSEE

WISDOM PUBLICATIONS
199 ELM ST
SOMERVILLE MA 02144-9908

Wisdom

WISDOM PUBLICATIONS

Please fill out and return this card if you would like to receive our catalogue and special offers. The postage is already paid!

NAME

ADDRESS

CITY / STATE / ZIP / COUNTRY

EMAIL

Sign up for our newsletter and special offers at wisdompubs.org

Wisdom Publications is a non-profit charitable organization.

The other thing to note is that Jesus, in instructing his disciples to recognize what is in their sight, suggests that such recognition comes from turning within. He is expressing belief in human beings' ability to achieve the same level of wisdom as he has himself. In fact, he implies that turning inward is the direction a truth seeker must always go. The Buddhist text the Udanavarga says that whoever sees what a wise man sees can also see the unseen, but whoever doesn't see the unseen does not perceive what he ought to see. In other words, if we develop the insight of the little child in saying 4, then we can see what most people do not, which is exactly what Jesus himself sees.

Case 2 of the *Record of Transmitting the Light*, a collection of koans with commentaries by Japanese Zen Master Keizan Jokin, states that we and the Buddha (in this case not the historical Buddha but the Cosmic Buddha or ultimate reality itself) always walk, stand, sit, and lie down together. Like the wave and the ocean, we are never separated even for an instant. If in this lifetime we don't see this, then we are not doing ourselves justice.

Unfortunately, most of us usually perceive only the partial picture, the surface reality, that is, the phenomenal aspect, and not the essential aspect. We see separation but not unity. Our intellect and our ego dominate so that we grow used to using them as the main ways in which we see reality. While this is useful and necessary, it can also impede intuitive and nonconceptual knowing via other channels.

Thus Jesus points to the fact that it is not just the intellectual or discriminating mind that should be engaged but also what we might call "big mind," the consciousness that can clearly reflect objects like a mirror. This is our primordial awareness that engages with things. It is what enables us to see what cannot be seen. It is accessed through meditation, contemplation, and trusting in the fruits of mental and physical solitude.

Some versions of saying 5 have Jesus saying "know what is before your face," which is another way of saying that truth is found within the now, within whatever position we find ourselves in. This operates in two ways—to see correctly and without ego whatever presents itself to us in our daily lives and to see properly that reality is both phenomenal and essential all at once.

What this requires is both attention to the present—what is in front of our face—and the free-flowing use of big mind. By doing this we can react quickly to circumstances in an appropriate and enlightened way. In this way all things can manifest themselves, and what was previously hidden will become plain to us. The irony, therefore, is that the "secret" meaning is the plain meaning.

This is the opposite of what we usually think. We think the secret meaning is some awesome and immense supramundane knowledge that will transform our lives and move us in the direction of the extraordinary. And in one way it does do that: to realize emptiness, or to see the face of the eternal, can't do otherwise. On the other hand, however, Matthew 11:25 suggests that what has been hidden from those that think they are wise and clever but has been revealed to children instead is that the immediacy of the now calls for clarity and practicality—the diaper needs changing and the milk needs to be warm. Or as someone from the Zen tradition might put it: eat when hungry, sleep when tired, this is the greatest wisdom.

Another version of saying 5 occurs as saying 17: "I'll give you what no eye has ever seen, no ear has ever heard, no hand has ever touched, and no human mind has ever thought." Even though Jesus states that he will "give" his disciples "what no eye has ever seen," the constant theme throughout *Thomas* is that this giving is the teaching and not enlightenment. Unless the disciples themselves recognize "what no eye has ever seen," "what no ear has ever heard," "what no hand has touched," and "what no human mind has ever thought," they will not understand that the teaching is synonymous with Jesus, who is equated with the Kingdom within and without.

The four negatives—the invisible, the inaudible, the intangible, and the unarisen—are similar to what is listed in the *Heart Sutra*, the preeminent sutra that succinctly presents Mahayana Buddhist doctrine. In this sutra the nature of the ultimate is described.

> All things are essentially empty—not born, not destroyed; not stained, not pure; without loss, without gain. Therefore in emptiness there is no form, sensation, perception, mental reaction, consciousness; no eye, ear, nose, tongue, body, mind, no color, sound, smell, taste, touch, object of thought; no seeing and so on to no thinking; no ignorance and also no ending of ignorance, and so on to no old age and death, and also no ending of old age and death; no suffering, cause of suffering, cessation, path; no wisdom and no attainment.

The deeper fact the disciples must realize is that there cannot be separate eyes, ears, and other physical attributes in the one. If everything is joined, there are no separate things set apart from each other. There is no separate "message" to give. The invisible, the inaudible, the intangible, and the unrisen refer not to some discrete set of facts hidden from our physical functions, but to that which requires the lenses of nonduality to be understood.

In Matthew 6:22 Jesus said, "The eye is the lamp of the body; so if your eye is clear, your whole body will be full of light." In Zen Buddhism this holistic awareness is known as "the single eye" or "the one eye." This is the metaphorical "third eye" in the forehead, also known as the "true Dharma eye." A person who sees all things with wisdom is said to have this feature. This is the natural freedom that arises out of an unhindered, clear, and exhaustive view of everything.

When the Buddha settled a dispute about the nature of reality for two young men, Vasennha and Bharadvaja, they felt compelled to cry out, "Now I know, it is like something overturned is reinstalled, something covered is made manifest, it is as the path is told to one who has lost his way, as an oil lamp was lit for those who have eyes to see." The disciples must do what these two did. They must let go of their precious conceptions and listen with the heart if they are to truly know the wordless, indescribable ultimate. Sayings 5 and 17 suggest to us that the "secret" is right in front of our eyes.

11

INTEGRATION

Jesus said, "Fortunate is the lion eaten by a human, for the lion becomes human. Unfortunate is the human eaten by a lion, for the human becomes lion.

—*Gospel of Thomas*, saying 7

Master Yunmen Wenyan asked the monks in his monastery to respond to the following statement: "I don't ask you about before the fifteenth day; bring me a phrase about after the fifteenth day." Yunmen himself answered in the monks' stead, "Every day is a good day."

—*Blue Cliff Record*, case 6

Saying 7, like all of the other sayings in *Thomas*, has both a surface and a deeper meaning. It concerns not only the proper placement of desire in life, but appropriate and advantageous ways in which our desires can be successfully consolidated and synthesized.

The first level of meaning is concerned with the literal acts of ingestion—who eats whom, and who becomes whom. But we can go deeper and hear the lion as a metaphor for something akin to what Buddhism calls a *klesha*. The term *klesha* refers to negative psychological tendencies that produce unwholesome actions that produce negative karma. In English *klesha* can be rendered as "vices, poisons, obstructions, affliction, impurities" or "defilements." All of these refer to some sort of obstruction or disturbance of the mind.

So if klesha rules a person (that is, the lion devours a man), then that man is not in control of his life and will create harmful karma, which leads to more and more suffering. On the other hand, should klesha be controlled or eliminated (the man devours the lion), then that man is fortunate and blessed because this results in wholesome actions.

However, it goes even deeper still. By itself, the above mentality can lead to split dualisms that do not profit the truth seeker at all. By this I mean battles between flesh and spirit, animal tendencies and human ones, base and pure instincts. This can lead to a feeling of guilt and a tendency toward self-judgment and self-hatred.

The salve to this sort of negative tendency is to see Jesus's deeper meaning. That is, it is not so much a clash of animal will versus human but of the human and animal becoming each other. Rather than seeing everything purely in terms of a strict hierarchy in which the status of man is above the lion, especially when he eats the lion (his klesha), we can look at it in terms of synthesis and integration. We take into ourselves the energy of the lion so that it becomes a part of us that we can transmute and transform.

Instead of crushing our negative habits and maintaining a constant state of vigilance, we focus on the fact that it is not so much that we must destroy them, but rather we should see their fundamental emptiness. That is, they have power over us only if we give it to them. After all, our negative tendencies are not permanent and substantial things. Thus, we can use them to our advantage when we want so long as the man and not the lion remains in control.

So, for example, anger can be used wholesomely if it leads us to protect a victim of bullying, while hurtful anger can be left dormant. In emptiness everything is available to the practitioner, both good and evil. It just depends on what we want to enact in our lives.

These sorts of distinctions are especially relevant when it comes to desire. We might imagine Buddhism advocates the complete elimination of all desires—but this is not strictly true.

Confusion surrounding desire comes from the fact that in the Buddha's time the word had many meanings, both positive and negative. However, as C. A. F. Rhys Davids points out, the one English word *desire* is made to do duty for no less than seventeen Pali words. So to say that "all suffering is based on desire" and "the solution to this is the complete cessation of all desire" is incorrect and simplistic because it treats every kind of desire as harmful.

In reality, the Buddha talked about two types of desire—sensory desire and the desire for enlightenment. If we eradicate all desire, even the desire for enlightenment, realization is impossible. So we don't have to automatically condemn these positive desires because they help us, and when we reach enlightenment, they no longer rule us anyway because we are no longer "working at" enlightenment, but rather we are it.

As the *Lotus Sutra* teaches, by awakening to our innate nature we can reach nirvana as an ordinary person. We don't have to be this amazing, serene, and perfect person; we just have to be whole. Since in emptiness the sufferings of birth and death, and ignorance and enlightenment, are inseparable, we don't need to extinguish something in order to attain something else. The potential for complete realization for all people involves the whole mind-body complex, and so our life here on this earth in its totality enables us to reach nirvana. There's no need to go somewhere special and create some special state of mind—we just have to be who we truly are.

Seen in this light, kleshas are not so much extinguished as either manipulated for virtuous purposes or never encouraged. This is an integrative approach to the lion (a klesha) within us in which we harness its positive qualities and deny its negative ones. Should the ego-self (lion) completely devour or crush the true self, then the ego and klesha reign supreme. If the ego-self (lion) is integrated into the true self (man) however, so that both exist at the same time, then both the lion and the man work together.

In *Thomas*, Jesus suggests a balanced middle way beyond the extremes of the little ego-self on the one hand and the true self on the other. We must not just stop at harmonizing the energies of both lion and man; we must go one step further to be truly living. To be a living one like Jesus, we must move beyond duality and nonduality, the individual and oneness—we must be whole. That whole includes but goes beyond just the recognition of emptiness and the phenomenal, the ego-self and the true self; otherwise we could be stuck in one or the other and miss the larger picture that is beyond both.

The *Ten Bulls* or *Ten Ox Herding Pictures* is a series of short poems and accompanying pictures used in Zen to illustrate the stages of progression toward realization, the recognition of unity, and the subsequent return into the world with a newfound integration of differentiation in oneness. The oxherd symbolizes the separate self and the ox, which stands for essential nature.

In these pictures an ox and oxherd are at first separate, but eventually the oxherd comes to realize his fundamental identity with essential nature. The second to last stage of his journey is the "solitary moon" stage, as summarized by this traditional prose.

> He is a solitary cloud wafting lightly along the mountain peaks;
> Clapping his hands he sings joyfully in the moonlight, but remember a last wall is still left barring his homeward walk.

This is the solitary one mentioned in saying 23—"I'll choose you, one out of a thousand and two out of ten thousand, and they'll stand as a single one"—the person who has joyfully realized that both self and reality are just constructs to be left behind.

But this is not the final stage because there is one more step to take on the Way. In the tenth and last stage the enlightened oxherd returns to ordinary living, whole and fully functioning. He enters the town marketplace, doing all of the commonplace things that everyone else does, and shares his enlightened life with everyone around him. This is the true Zen "man of no rank."

The crucial unspoken question the living Jesus leaves the disciples with is what will they do now? It is not enough to be a disciple, we must be light itself; we must act from our new wholeness in every moment. That is the difference between someone who merely lives the religious life and a buddha, an awakened one. So when the lion and the man merge, what happens then? You can almost hear the disciples getting to the end of the saying and asking, "and then we . . . ?"

This is similar in a sense to case 6 of the *Blue Cliff Record*. In this koan Master Yunmen Wenyan, a major Chinese Zen master in Tang-era China, "asks the monks in his monastery to respond to the following statement: 'I don't ask you about before the fifteenth day; bring me a phrase about after the fifteenth day.' Yunmen himself answered in the monks' stead, 'Every day is a good day.' "

During Yunmen's time, the fifteenth of the month was considered a symbol of enlightenment because it was associated with the rising of the full moon—so what Yunmen is asking his students to consider is what it is like after we see our true self. "Bring me a phrase about after the fifteenth day" is asking how we will live our life after we have opened our eyes. Will we continue to gain insight and manifest wisdom in our lives or will we rest on our laurels and seek no further? Will we think just about individual "good" and "bad" days or will we also see each day as the absolute now? At that point, will we then consolidate both into a complete wholeness?

Saying 7 is talking about the middle way—what life is like when we fully integrate two things—what we saw before and what we saw after we opened our eyes. It is not enough for the man to integrate the lion in a wholesome way; the man must then make his way in life in the same manner as the living Jesus.

12

THE TREASURE CHAMBER

Jesus said, "The kingdom can be compared to someone who had a treasure [hidden] in their field. [They] didn't know about it. After they died, they left it to their son. The son didn't know it either. He took the field and sold it. The buyer plowed the field, [found] the treasure, and began to loan money at interest to whomever they wanted."

—*Gospel of Thomas*, saying 109

The treasure chamber opens by itself, and one uses the treasure at will.

—Eihei Dogen, "Fukanzazengi"

Here, the *Gospel of Thomas* emphasizes that to strike to the heart of realization and embody the life of a living one, we must make the right choices when opportunities present themselves. It is only by putting aside what is not profitable and completely investing in what is truly valuable that we can come to the clear and discriminating insight of realization. If we do not make this choice, then the Kingdom—our essential nature—remains closed to us.

Saying 109 cuts to the chase immediately with a simile: The Kingdom is like a man who had a hidden treasure in his field. This man is not wise because unlike those with spiritual development, he cannot see true wealth, and so in the course of his ordinary life he cannot make good choices. He does not live up to his full potential. Without seeing the treasure and recognizing it for what it is, and then choosing it above all else, he stays undeveloped and ignorant. This treasure is his essential nature. The message, then, is that only those who first see the real treasure and then make the leap into the ultimate will be able to reap the rewards of clear seeing. All other things are small fry in comparison and not essential to escaping the taste of death.

The parable of the burning house in the *Lotus Sutra* tells us a story about a fire that begins to consume a house in which there are children. Outside the house, the father realizes that decisive action must be taken. He thinks of reasoning with the children but sees that they are too busy playing with their toys. So he calls out to them that they should come out of the house and play with the wonderful carts he has for them— and this is enough to make the children leave the house and escape the fire.

In this parable, the father realizes that these children are not truly satisfied with the toys they have. The enjoyment of material things only goes so far. He knows that what they really need is the white bullock cart, that is, the ability to rest in their essential nature. He gives this to each of them. This wisdom, according to Daijian Huineng, the sixth ancestor of Zen, teaches us to dispense with the makeshift and to resort to the ultimate. When we do that, we will appreciate that we are the sole owner of these valuables and we can use its treasures at will. When you are free, he suggests, from the idea that the wish-fulfilling gem belongs only to someone else, then you have learned the right way to live.

The clincher is to recognize the true treasure whenever and in whatever way it presents itself and then make a decisive move. The buyer who came to plow the field and found the treasure while working used it immediately. This presents the correct and wise response. Perishable goods and false riches can't be compared to the unfailing and enduring treasure that the world cannot destroy. The plowman saw this immediately. While *Thomas* usually takes a dim view of commerce and the trappings of material wealth, in this case, it is put to metaphorical good use.

In traditional interpretations of the canonical Gospels, Jesus is sometimes referred to as the "pearl of great price"—a jewel of inestimable value. An awakened life is not just worth a priceless pearl; it *is* the pearl. In the Zen tradition a similar term, the "one bright pearl," came about through the enlightenment experience of Zen Master Xuansha Shibei. In lay life he enjoyed fishing and used to ply his boat on the nearby river, following the fishermen. Master Eihei Dogen comments that no doubt he did not expect the golden fish—essential nature or realization—that comes of itself without fishing for it.

Xuansha never read the sutras, the worldly treasures of Zen, but one day he stubbed his toe accidentally and realized the Way. He exclaimed, "The whole universe is the one bright pearl." The one bright pearl goes by many names—oneness, emptiness, buddha nature, essential nature, true self, the ultimate, the cosmic Jesus, and the Cosmic Buddha. These labels all stand for a unified tranquility that is never lost.

In saying 109 the importance of the discovery of our own true identity is contrasted with those who, like the person who had a treasure hidden in his field but did not know it, are ignorant of a deeper side to life. This is also like the gem hidden in the shirt of a drunken man in a classic Zen story. In this story a rich man places a jewel in his friend's shirt, thinking to help his down-and-out companion who, in his sorrow, had drunken too much and passed out. When the rich man met his friend many years later, he was still down and out. He had completely missed the jewel. He was ignorant of the fact that essential nature is the gem inside all of us.

If we do not recognize our essential nature, we cannot live up to our ever-present potential. The *Surangama Sutra* points out that not knowing our essential nature is comparable to a man who seeks after food when he has a treasure in his own storehouse. In saying 109 both the father and his son are like this. They are ignorant of their true worth and of the fact that, as the *Flower Ornament Sutra* observes, "the awakened mind is like a good field for it nurtures all good phenomena." They do not put any effort into reaping true wealth.

Only the third owner of the field, who toils in the field with his plow, is deserving of treasure. The implication of saying 109 is that we must dig beneath the surface to find the treasure. We must dig up the dirt and unsettle our attachments and concepts to discover what they are obscuring. Just buying the land is not enough: we must work for the meal of enlightenment. The groundwork is not just in relation to the field but the heart and mind as well.

In the Pali Canon, the standard collection of scriptures in early Buddhism, there is a story in which the farmer Kasi Bharadvaja sees the Buddha begging for alms and says, "You claim to be a plowman, but I don't see your plowing." He's a little peeved at the monks because he thinks they do nothing. The Buddha answered: "Faith is the seed, austerities the rain, wisdom my yoke and plow, conscientiousness the pole, mind the reins, and mindfulness is my driving stick."

In saying 109 the original landowner is not rich but ignorant of his birthright, while the new landowner transforms himself from spiritually poor to spiritually cultivated by working on what should be worked on. According to the Buddha, this is the mark of an awakened person. When he himself was asked about this subject, he said, "I have cultivated what should be cultivated, and dispelled what should be dispelled, therefore I'm enlightened."

Of course, this is not the end of the story. In saying 109, not only recognizing and choosing the essential self is crucial, but one must also return to the world and use that newfound knowledge with others. The wisdom and prudence of a living one are further emphasized in saying 109 since it is now not enough just for the disciples to know themselves but to make their entire lives reflect that knowledge.

This way of life is expressed in a koan drawn from the writings of Dogen: "The treasure chamber opens by itself, and one uses the treasure at will." Since the Way is all-pervading, it is the ever-available treasure-house that we can draw from. A realized person will try to use this wealth in every moment, not only for themselves but for others as well. Rather than resting on our laurels, we use our newfound understanding in our daily lives.

Thus the farmer, after discovering his treasure, lends at interest. *Thomas* strongly warns against usury, so at first glance this seems at odds with other sayings. If we regard the lending as a spiritual metaphor, however, this discordance is dissolved because "to loan money at interest to whomever they wanted" is the metaphorical communication of knowledge, the free flow of insight to and between people. The farmer does not withhold his knowledge. Rather, he shares it with those who are in need of wisdom but do not yet have enough to secure it.

Sharing wisdom in this way is the teaching of a living one. This kind of person seeks repayment in the development of insight in the "borrower" so that they become free from debt, and even have a surplus to continue their own good work, thereby spreading the Word. The failure of the first two men to discover their treasure, with the success only of the third, also lends itself to the idea that unless we look for the treasure in our own field, we will never profit from it. Saying 109 warns us that if we want to profit from wisdom, then we must engage with what we know and use it in our interactions with others.

13

Our Time Is Now

Jesus said, "Often you've wanted to hear this message that I'm telling you, and you don't have anyone else from whom to hear it. There will be days when you'll look for me, but you won't be able to find me."

—*Gospel of Thomas*, saying 38

Let me respectfully remind you: Life and Death are of supreme importance. Time swiftly passes by and opportunity is lost. Each of us should strive to awaken. Take heed. Do not squander your life.

—*Evening Gatha*, chanted each night of Zen retreat

In saying 38 Jesus seems intent on urging his disciples to develop a sense of the now, that the path is not reserved for some time in the far future. He admonishes them with these words: "Often you've wanted to hear this message that I'm telling you, and you don't have anyone else from whom to hear it. There will be days when you'll look for me, but you won't be able to find me."

This is very similar to the Buddha's last words in the *Maha Parinibbana Sutta*:

Then the Buddha addressed the monks: "It may be, that even a single brother may be in doubt or uncertainty about the Buddha or the doctrine or the path or the course of conduct. Ask, brethren; do not with regret say afterwards, 'The master was face to face with us, and we could not ask him face to face' . . . Well then, brethren, I now exhort you. Impermanent are compound things; strive with earnestness." These were the last words of the Buddha.

Time waits for no one—especially those who do not take advantage of circumstances or don't pay attention to where they're at. Like the Buddha, Jesus realized that there were some people who had squandered their time with him and did not understand his message. They looked outside themselves and to Jesus for the answer instead of looking within.

On a surface level this saying means that Jesus can't be seen because the disciples will no longer be dependent upon these sayings. Seeking in the text becomes redundant to those who have achieved understanding. There is more to this, however, than redundant text.

As is usual with *Thomas*, an extra meaning is contained within the saying and that is that eventually the disciples must come to recognize that the Kingdom is both within and without. This means that there is no separate person to realize wisdom, and no separate wisdom to obtain. They might seek for the individual "thing" known as Jesus, but ultimately they will not find him. They will find only oneness.

To seek for Jesus and not find him challenges us in the same way that koans do, presenting information not accessible by the intellect. So not only will there be a time when Jesus is not physically around, but also a person who is truly enlightened sees that in the one there is no separate Jesus, disciple, eye, ear, nose, body, or consciousness to be found anyway. The koan of "not finding Jesus" is the essential task of saying 38.

It is also the warning of saying 59 in which Jesus cautions the disciples to take heed of the living one while you are alive, lest you die and seek to see him and be unable to do so. Here Jesus is not talking about the metaphorical death of the small ego-self but the actual death of the physical entities known as "disciples." It is not Jesus's physical disappearance from the world but their own that they must use to spur them on to freedom.

Both of these sayings cry out the very same thing that Majjhima Nikaya 27 does: "Do not die filled with longing. To die filled with longing is painful." As Sutta Nipata 4.2 tells us, it is a sorry state of affairs that sometimes it is only death that brings a realization of endings, and then a person enmeshed in his senses, deeply immersed in the body, will shout: "What will happen to me after death?" It is no good waiting until the time of death to inquire into the nature of the Kingdom only to find you come up short.

Saying 38 tells us that time is ticking away. We cannot realize the deathless after we have died because by then it is too late. If we do not trust ourselves sufficiently, Zen Master Linji Yixuan warns us, we will be completely anxious, pursuing all sorts of things and being changed by them, unable to be independent. Saying 38 tells us that either we trust our own nature and work on knowing the Kingdom or we reject it and be manipulated by outside forces.

14

Dependent Origination

Jesus said, "Look, a sower went out, took a handful of seeds, and scattered them. Some fell on the roadside; the birds came and gathered them. Others fell on the rock; they didn't take root in the soil and ears of grain didn't rise toward heaven. Yet others fell on thorns; they choked the seeds and worms ate them. Finally, others fell on good soil; it produced fruit up toward heaven, some sixty times as much and some a hundred and twenty."

—*Gospel of Thomas*, saying 9

The Buddha-seed germinates through dependent origination. All the suffering and joy we experience depend on conditions. If we should be blessed by some great reward, such as fame or fortune, it's the fruit of a seed planted by us in the past. When conditions change, it ends. Why delight in its existence? But while success and failure depend on conditions, the mind neither waxes nor wanes.

—*Lotus Sutra*, chapter 2

Saying 9 speaks of the wonderful transformation that arises from both good and wise actions (no matter how small) and the natural workings of our essential nature. To this is added a caveat: it is more profitable to be careful about where we place the seed of wisdom in order to make use of the right conditions for germination.

Moreover, the growth of this divine seed is dependent upon the state of receptivity in the heart-mind of the recipient. The theme of hearing with the heart and seeing with the wisdom eye is constantly and consistently repeated. The deeper meaning of these sayings, then, is that the world (and enlightenment) proceeds according to dependent origination—the interplay of causes and conditions.

Saying 9 describes a scenario in which a person, the sower, gathers many seeds and scatters them on four types of ground: the road, the rocky ground, among thorns, and on good soil. The first three fail to produce a good harvest while the last produces two different yields, 60 and 120 times as much as the original seeds.

As with all of the sayings, the surface meaning, that of farming, is not the intended meaning. The sower can represent many things—Jesus, an enlightened person, or the sayings themselves. It is anything that sparks the seed of wisdom in a person. While living ones give teachings, they can show the way only since it is the responsibility of everyone to grow the wisdom seed within. One way to do that is make the teachings accessible so that people can use them if they so desire.

Since the sower has abundant seed, enough to fill his hand, it is clear that he has germinated the Word within himself and is now attempting to give something that will in turn propagate wisdom in others. Out of compassion for the world, those who have become the tree of life feel themselves tasked with increasing the yield of awareness and so seek to find receptive and fertile ground.

Jesus taught many people in many places and even found the desert conducive to his own insight. Likewise, while it may appear that the sower is either a hopeless farmer or unaware of the necessary conditions for high-yield crops, he decides to distribute seed in places not normally associated with successful farming. Rather than randomness or a lack of judgment, he does this, the Samyutta Nikaya tells us, because "even ignorant people, if they were to understand even a single sentence that would be a blessing and a happiness for them for a long time."

The world already has the potential to produce results, and the seed can be sown anywhere. Wisdom can sprout in any place because there is nowhere that is not infused with divine energy. Understanding this is to fully realize dependent origination—that everything feeds into and contributes to everything else. This means that no one is separate from or outside the range of cause and effect. Should we hear the teachings and meditate upon them, the ultimate will reply.

Since everything is interlinked in emptiness, the universe responds to a person because it is not separate from that person. This is why the *Lotus Sutra* makes a point of stressing that the "Buddha-seed germinates through dependent origination." The implication of this is that the disciples must develop their essential nature and nurture their insight if they wish to truly benefit. They must develop certain characteristics associated with the wise. Our own mind is like a field, and performing virtuous and wise actions is like sowing good seeds in that field.

In Buddhism a *buddha-field* is any place that is a pure manifestation of wisdom, while sowing the seeds of wisdom through good deeds, conduct, service, and teaching to others makes them our *field of merit*. This field is of benefit to both the teacher and the learner and the solid ground from which awakening grows.

The lessons of saying 9 are many. As we travel the road of awareness, we must not be hardhearted, sealed off so that nothing can penetrate our defenses. The good sower may plant the good seeds of wisdom, but if we do not make judicious use of them, they do not come to fruition. Instead, they die, thus making way for seeds of a dubious nature. So it's of no use just to listen for a moment and then forget what we heard. While we may receive the teachings with joy in the moment, if wisdom can't take root deeply within then when we are tested our spiritual sight becomes dim. If we also allow ourselves to be overwhelmed during the ups and downs of this world, then a thorny and insidious negativity overcomes us. Our intellect and doubts work away at whatever sense of groundedness we may have developed. We might retain and understand things, but when it comes time for wise action, which is also the fruit, adventitious defilements stifle it.

To add to this, our ego and its narcissistic attachments may also worm their way into our consciousness. Yet there is hope, and it lies in nurturing virtue, developing ennobling habits of mind and action, and clearly understanding the Kingdom within. This is the good soil that reaps the benefit of tender and constant care. It is also the realization that the Word thrives due to dependent origination—the right causes and conditions.

There is no ill will in the birds eating the seed; it's what birds naturally do. Thorns become entangled in things, and worms, being worms, eat away at whatever nourishment they can find. Even if we do interpret the worm as a symbol of evil and thorns as the delusions that grow in and through us, cause and effect still operates. Again, we return to the theme of not tasting death through persistence in seeking, finding, and then applying what we have learned.

Galatians 6:7 points out that a person harvests whatever he plants. The Buddhist version of "reap what you sow" is the *Samuddaka Sutta*. This says that whatever seeds you sow, you carry away their fruits. If we sow a pure stock of seeds, we will get good quality fruit.

Bitter seeds from the neem tree, bitter cucumber, and the sponge gourd, the Buddha explained, will never produce appetizing fruit because they only produce fruit with an unpleasant taste. Similarly, wrong conduct will not produce a good effect. The seeds of sugar cane and fragrant rice, however, will produce sweet sugar and delicious grains. Similarly, good conduct will only produce a good effect: someone who does good things will get good results and a person who does not will not.

Again, Jesus is pointing within. He is asking the disciples to see that if they truly knew the Kingdom then this would be reflected in their actions and state of mind. To create a store of good we must create it within the heart-mind, since all else flows from that. If that place denies the living Jesus, then a person cannot live in the way in which they were meant to.

This idea of a storehouse can be further explained by the notion of the *alaya-vijnana* or "storehouse consciousness" of the Yogacara school of Mahayana Buddhism. Within us, this school maintains, is a storage consciousness that contains all the impressions of previous experiences. Since it contains the seeds of various types of karma, it is the storehouse of habitual tendencies that we have cultivated over time. Since these are likely to enter our consciousness at any time and affect our actions, we "water" the good seeds with insight and deny the evil ones any sustenance. They wither away or are rendered harmless.

The lesson of this saying is the same as Udanavarga 9.8: "Whatever a person does, whether it's virtuous or not, there are none that are of little importance. They all bear some kind of fruit." The unproductive seed and the good seed are metaphors for the uneccessary and the necessary features of a good life. Saying 9 tells us that to learn to tell the difference between these is crucial to living in a fully realized way.

15

THE FIRE OF WISDOM

Jesus said, "I've cast fire on the world, and look, I'm watching over it until it blazes."

— *Gospel of Thomas*, saying 10

Just because it is so clear, it takes us longer to realize it. If you quickly acknowledge that the candlelight is fire, you will find that the rice has long been cooked.

— *Gateless Gate*, case 7

Saying 10 emphasizes that to awaken the Kingdom within we must be ready to sacrifice our attachments and create a unity that sees no division. To do this we must enter the fire of the Kingdom and burn that which can be burned, while preserving and encouraging insight into the eternal. To be near or in the fire of Jesus is to awaken, but to be far from it is to remain in delusion.

In Buddhist texts there are numerous comparisons between the ways in which a fire and a mind work. The unawakened mind is said to be like a burning fire of delusions; the awakened mind, like a fire gone out. *Nirvana* itself means "having been blown out." While fire as a symbol for delusions dominates the sutras, it is also recognized that in itself fire is neutral; it is how we use it that is prejudicial.

Fire can either burn with delusion as its fuel, or it can burn away delusion. Anyone is capable of nurturing the good fire of an awakened mind or of putting out the mind ablaze with adventitious defilements. In the Buddha's time society was divided into several different castes from high to low. When questioned by a man of the upper caste why the Buddha thought actions both good and bad are committed across all castes (not just the "good" ones), the Buddha replied that all fire has the same flame, color, and luster, and it is possible to do whatever work that has to be done with it. In other words, the fire of diligence, insight, and good works is available to anyone who seeks awakening. It is eternally available because our essential nature is eternal.

In the koan "Zhaozhou Washes His Bowl" (*Gateless Gate*, case 7) Master Zhaozhou Congshen, a Zen master especially known for his straightforward manner of teaching, described a foolish man who once searched for fire with a lit lantern. Zhaozhou wryly observed that had he known what fire was, he could have cooked his rice much sooner— that is, he would have realized the jewel of his true nature was with him all along.

Noting the need for conscientiousness and diligence, the Buddha also likened the fire of wisdom to the fire made by a person skilled in starting and maintaining fires. Earnest seekers, like a skilled fire maker, must work hard to start and keep the fire going. Only when it reaches maturity are we able to use the fire (wisdom) in the way we want.

So having sparked the fire of transformational wisdom through his teaching, Jesus is "watching over it until it blazes." To burn away delusions and replace them with the solitary fire of nondual consciousness there must be conscious mindfulness of our own speech, body, and mind. Jesus is encouraging his disciples to build their own fire of wisdom, since he knew what the Buddha knew, that "those who delight in heedfulness and look with fear at heedlessness advance like fire, burning all fetters, small and large." In the meantime, Jesus is tending the wisdom teachings until the disciples catch fire themselves.

In Zen the fire of wisdom is likened to the ambrosia that brings satisfaction and to a lamp whose light cannot be obscured. Zen Master Jianfu Chenggu once remarked that the experience of being on a religious path is like hiding your body in fire—it melts everything. To have "cast a fire upon the world" is to have taught the wisdom that burns away separation between the disciples and the Kingdom. This fire is not the cataclysmic and instantaneous fire of Judgment Day or a time predicted in the Anguttara Nikaya "when the vast world will burn up, being completely destroyed and ceasing to exist." It is the present fire of wisdom in the seeker that starts small and needs protection and care until it matures.

Once we have seen emptiness, our true nature blazes away unimpededly. It can then be consciously "entered into" and the deathless attained. The *Mahaparinirvana Sutra* describes how the Buddha, after having kindled and maintained the fire of wisdom in himself, announced, "I proceed burning bright like a flame."

In saying 82, the twin companion to saying 10, Jesus reinforces this necessity of burning away separation between ourselves and the Kingdom: "Whoever is near me is near the fire, and whoever is far from me is far from the kingdom." In saying 10 he cast a fire in order to emphasize that it must become the task of each individual to fuel their own. In saying 82 he *is* the fire, and so distance from Jesus is distance from the Kingdom. To maintain distance is to foster the separate self, but to be near the fire is to be close to the true self. Actually being within the fire is uniting with it. The deeper meaning in this saying is that it is only by completely burning away the separate self that we can be transformed.

In Mahayana Buddhism fire is traditionally held to be one of the four great elements (in addition to earth, water, and wind) that make up the cosmos. The nature of fire is heat, so it can bring things to perfection. In some Buddhist rituals, fire is said to symbolize the wisdom of enlightenment that burns away any defilements. To be near the fire or within the fire is likened to becoming wisdom itself.

Zen Master Wumen Huikai, compiler of and commentator on the *Gateless Gate*, suggested that we must exhaust every ounce of energy we have in doing this. If we do not give up on the Way, we will be enlightened in the same way that an altar candle is lit by one touch of the match. In case 2 of the *Record of Transmitting the Light*, Venerable Mahakashyapa, known as "Light Bringer" and one of the wisest disciples of the Buddha, excitedly stated that realization was just like "fire uniting with fire." The true self knows itself.

Since the kind of understanding Jesus is talking about requires complete nonattachment, to be near the fire that is Jesus is a necessity for awakening, since only it has enough power to cut through delusions. To eliminate the distance between Jesus (the wisdom fire) and ourselves is what is required for awakening. The unity of the essential world means that "near" and "far" are delusions. By entering into the fire and then becoming that fire, conceptual separation completely disappears, and we fully enter the Kingdom. It is only by burning the flammable parts that the nonflammable parts are laid bare. What is it that cannot be burned? What cannot be extinguished is a living one's pearl of great price, their essential nature.

Sayings 10 and 82 contain instructions and lessons for "making the two into one." The person who goes through this process "stands solitary" (further discussed in saying 23). They become an *ihidaya*, a "single unified one," which is a Syriac-Aramaic term for an enlightened person who operates within a nondual consciousness. To see Jesus, then, is to see the whole truth, and to see the truth is to know ourselves as whole. To be divided within ourselves or to have a divided community runs contrary to the natural unity of the ultimate.

16

THE PHILOSOPHERS
AND ZEN SICKNESS

Jesus said to his disciples, "If you were to compare me to someone, who would you say I'm like?" Simon Peter said to him, "You're like a just angel." Matthew said to him, "You're like a wise philosopher." Thomas said to him, "Teacher, I'm completely unable to say whom you're like." Jesus said, "I'm not your teacher. Because you've drunk, you've become intoxicated by the bubbling spring I've measured out." He took him aside and told him three things. When Thomas returned to his companions, they asked, "What did Jesus say to you?" Thomas said to them, "If I tell you one of the things he said to me, you'll pick up stones and cast them at me, and fire will come out of the stones and burn you up."

—*Gospel of Thomas*, saying 13

The wisteria withers, the tree falls down, the mountain collapses; The water roaring in the valley—fire sparkling from the whirling stones.

—*Record of Transmitting the Light*, case 2

Saying 13 uses the imagery and metaphor of drinking from a well to represent the acquisition of insight into the nature of the Kingdom. It points out that failure to do this means a failure to live up to the potential of our own nature since it creates an unassailable and unnecessary division between the ultimate and us.

There are many potential stopping-off points along the road to enlightenment, and each disciple in these sayings represents varying profitable and unprofitable stages of insight. Only Thomas, the sayings stress, truly understands the Kingdom, and it is he whom we should emulate.

In saying 13, Jesus says to his disciples, "Compare me to someone and tell me whom I am like." Simon Peter gives one answer ("you are like a just angel"), Matthew another ("you are like a wise philosopher"), and finally Thomas gives his ("Teacher, I'm completely unable to say whom you're like"). Jesus rebukes Thomas: "I'm not your teacher. Because you've drunk, you've become intoxicated by the bubbling spring I've measured out."

The first question is similar to a *sassho* (checking question) used by Zen teachers. These questions perform two functions. First, they confirm a student's insight into the eternal and gauge the depth of that insight. Second, they push the student to broaden their insight beyond oneness into particular instances of it. For example, the now-famous koan "The Sound of One Hand" is typically followed by checking questions such as "What is the sound of one hand in the forest or in the ocean?"

This method is a way of checking the depth and quality of a person's understanding. Since it puts someone on the spot, it does not give them a chance to prepare a response, so if any answer shows hesitation or awkwardness then it is not naturally arising from what they already know. In the case of saying 13 Jesus gives the checking question, "If you were to compare me to someone, who would you say I'm like?"

On the surface this looks like Jesus is requesting the disciples to categorize and encapsulate him in a quick reply. On a deeper level, he is ascertaining whether the disciples have discerned the fact that ultimately there is no distinction between Jesus and anyone else. The Kingdom is all things, and it transforms the "two into one." Saying 108 states that whoever drinks from Jesus becomes like him and Jesus becomes that person. To compare the Kingdom to the Kingdom cannot be done. The question seeks to circumvent logic and intellection and prompt an answer that comes from the "hidden" knowledge revealed to them.

Jesus quickly sees that there are differences among the levels of realization of these disciples, and he reacts differently to them. To the first two, Peter and Matthew, he does not reply. Neither does he deny that he is their messiah or teacher. Their discernment is conventional, linear, and superficial, and it would be of no use to enter into something deeper with them. Rather than come to an understanding of the Christ within, they can only perceive that it is the actual "words" of Jesus and his incarnated personage that will deliver them.

Peter conceives of Jesus only as the messiah, someone who will give him wisdom or show him the way. The drawback of this is that Peter looks without rather than within for the source of his liberation, when in fact he needs to reach the point where, like the lay follower Nandaka when he realized the meaning of the Buddha's words, he feels compelled to shout "Enough, I say, with this external bath. I am satisfied with this internal bath."

Matthew likens Jesus to a philosopher. Like Peter, he denies the limitless nature of the Kingdom by measuring Jesus and placing him into a definitive category. By doing this he does not understand that the sayings' deeper features can only be seen without paying any attention whatsoever to explicit formulations of text. No system of thought and no amount of theoretical understanding can communicate its true meaning because truth is to be experienced. It cannot be fully realized through theories.

This is due to the fact that the intellect is not the highest level of reality. In the Digha Nikaya the Buddha observed that this means philosophers can be entrapped in "the net of philosophical speculation; this way and that they may flounder, but they are included in it and caught in it." Moreover, it is not advisable to believe something just because it matches our own philosophy for our own hubris may be at play.

A well-known Zen story concerns Sada Kaiseki, a learned Japanese Buddhist scholar, who was once at a loss to distinguish Buddhism from the assertions of Indian astronomy. He taxed his reason to the utmost to demonstrate the Buddhist theory and at the same time to refute the Copernican theory.

One day he called on Zen Master Yeki-do, the abbot of the Soji-ji Monastery, one of two head temples of the Soto school of Zen, and explained the construction and characteristics of the universe as described in the sutras, saying that Buddhism would come to nothing if the Buddhist conception was overthrown by the Copernican. Master Yeki-do exclaimed: "Buddhism aims to destroy concepts of the cosmos and to establish Buddha's holy kingdom throughout the universe. Why do you waste your energy in the construction of the universe according to the sutras?"

In other words, the wisdom of the Buddha is to consider philosophical concepts but not to believe in their infallibility. To hold them as the primary truth is a fetter and the cause of wrong view. The sacred text of Zen is not of paper but one written in heart and mind.

The *Lankavatara Sutra* sums it up succinctly: the fundamental delusion of those caught in the net of philosophical views is that they do not recognize that the objective world rises from the one mind itself; they do not understand that the whole mind-system also arises from the mind itself. Instead, they continue to cherish the dualism of this and that, of being and nonbeing, ignorant of the fact that there is but one common essence. They do not comprehend that enlightenment is not something to be grasped in terms of doctrine or philosophical concept or system.

Thomas, however, recognizes the larger picture—since Jesus is the Kingdom, we can view this as the eternal speaking when he speaks. In John 7:16 Jesus himself pointed out that "what I teach doesn't come from me." His ineffability is Thomas's focus. Thomas transcends the student-master dichotomy and instead becomes the Kingdom, the living Jesus. Like anyone else who attains the deathless, he transforms into Jesus's "twin brother." The word *didymos* is Greek for "twin," and *Thomas* is Aramaic for "twin." So Didymos Judas Thomas is a twin in more than one way—he is the mirror image of the living Jesus, the Kingdom.

The three disciples represent the kind of differentiation that can be found among seekers in the wisdom traditions. An illustration of this is in the *Jingde Records of the Transmission of the Lamp*. Bodhidharma, the first Chinese ancestor of Zen, once asked a checking question of his disciples. "Can each of you say something to demonstrate your understanding?"

Dao Fu stepped forward and said, "It is not bound by words and phrases, nor is it separate from words and phrases." Bodhidharma said, "You have attained my skin." The nun Zong Chi stepped up and said, "It is like a glorious glimpse of the realm of Akshobhya Buddha. Seen once, it need not be seen again." Bodhidharma said, "You have attained my flesh." Dao Yu said, "Not a single thing can be grasped." Bodhidharma said, "You have attained my bones." Finally, Dazu Huike came forth, bowed deeply in silence and stood up straight. Bodhidharma said, "You have attained my marrow." Bodhidharma passed on the symbolic robe and bowl of succession to Dazu Huike.

In John 6:53 Jesus says to the crowd gathered around him, "I say to you, unless you eat the flesh of the Son of Man and drink his blood, you have no life in you." Similarly, in the Bodhidharma example, the metaphors of skin, flesh, bones, and marrow reflect varying points along a continuum ranging from superficial to enlightened. They allow us to gain a sense of where a person is in their understanding.

The first student, Dao Fu, is like Peter: he speaks of something outside of himself—in this case words and letters—thereby denying immanence. We all need words and teachers to convey something, but they are not ends in themselves. Zong Chi sees the eternal like a messiah: it comes once from upon high. Dao Yu's "not a single thing can be grasped" sees that everything is the Kingdom, but is still relying on words to express that. Lastly, as with saying 13's silent "three things," Huike's spontaneous and silent expression of mystery says all that needs to be said.

The radical egalitarianism of the *Gospel of Thomas*, like the Zen lineage into which Dazu Huike was accepted, promises spiritual evolution. Saying 108 presents the facts—provided one fully embodies the wisdom of the sayings, there is a reciprocity of divine knowledge between us and Jesus. This equivalency means that both Jesus and Thomas are sons of the living Father. Thomas initially accepts the authority of Jesus as teacher because Jesus knows his true self. When Thomas comes to know the same thing, the authority is shared and personal. Jesus as teacher has disappeared.

In Zen Buddhism, realization of one's own true nature is not in order to become a "special" person but rather an ordinary, plain person who fully integrates their understanding into their life. Like Jesus in the *Gospel of Thomas*, a Zen teacher does not teach in order to display the magnitude of their own insight but to help a student know what the teacher knows, to attain an equal but individual recognition of the eternal.

The *Gateless Gate* states that those who have passed the barrier of the separate ego-self are able not only to see Master Zhaozhou Congshen (the greatest Zen master of Tang dynasty China) face to face, but also to walk hand in hand with the whole descending line of ancestors and be eyebrow to eyebrow with them. We will see with the same eye that they see with and hear with the same ear that they hear with.

When a student questioned the sixth ancestor of Zen, Daijian Huineng, whether there was any further secret idea besides the mystery just spoken by him, he replied, "What I have told you is no secret. If you reflect inwardly, the secret is in you." The student commented, "Now that I have received your instruction I am like a man who takes a drink of water and knows for himself whether it is cold or warm."

Despite Jesus recognizing Thomas's depth of wisdom, however, he still chides him by rejecting the title of "Teacher." *Teacher* suggests that

Thomas still thinks in terms of division. Jesus nevertheless continues and affirms that Thomas's understanding is correct but needs a little more to be fully mature. Thomas's "I'm completely unable to say whom you're like" is equivalent to Dao Yu's "not a single thing can be grasped." It is the truth, but eight words too many for the ineffable.

So while Thomas has drunk freely from Jesus's bubbling spring as he was supposed to do, Jesus describes him as "intoxicated." He has imbibed wisdom, but the experience has created too much of an ethereal state of mind. By going into the larger mind, or big mind as I mentioned in the discussion of saying 5, he is drunk with insight. In Zen this is known as Zen sickness.

Case 11, "Yunmen's Two Diseases," from the *Book of Equanimity*, gives a description of Zen sickness. In this koan Master Yunmen Wenyan states that there are two sicknesses concerning the dharmakaya. One is when you have had an enlightenment experience but still hang on to it, and another is when you think that one bit of insight is all you have to attain.

When someone gains insight into the Kingdom, they can fall prey to the idea that that's all they need to do, that further practice is not needed. Overwhelmed, they can be satisfied with a state of pure joy and amazement. The "stink" of the separate self who has "gained" enlightenment persists.

Thomas is like this. He knows the ineffable is not describable in words but Jesus sees that he must take a further step and come down to earth, to clear the air of realization as a "thing" instead of one's natural way of operating in the world. This is why when Master Zhaozhou Congshen asked Nanquan Puyuan, "What is the Path?" he replied, "The ordinary mind is the Path."

Jesus's response is to take Thomas aside and have a quiet word with him. He says three things that prompt Thomas to come back to the ground from his attainment. In a koanlike manner the saying does not tell us what these three things are but invites us to consider and contemplate them. They are mysterious but serve the purpose of what in Zen is known as "turning words."

Turning words are phrases designed to prompt us to full realization, to fall off the edge of any delusion that may still linger. They are the words upon which the point of the student-teacher encounter "turns," and they carry the power to turn the mind of participants, audience, or reader. The most well-known examples of turning words in Zen Buddhism are case 100, "The Three Turning Words of Baling Haojian," and case 96, "Zhaozhou's Three Turning Words," from the *Blue Cliff Record*. In Zhaozhou's case they are: (1) a clay Buddha cannot pass through water; (2) a wooden Buddha cannot pass through fire; and (3) a metal Buddha cannot pass through a furnace. Each of these is designed to enable a student to see the truth of reality.

If a Buddha of clay were to pass through water, a wooden Buddha through fire, and a metal one through a furnace, they would disintegrate. However, if they do not pass through, then they remain as they are—untransformed. To die to self and live again they must somehow pass through the barriers and become illuminated by the true fact, their essential self. In saying 13 Thomas must fully pass through the fire of the Kingdom and come out the other side to completely understand and embody it. Jesus is giving him a last push to do this.

This draws comparison to saying 7: "Fortunate is the lion eaten by a human, for the lion becomes human." We can also look at saying 13 through the lenses of synthesis and integration. We take into ourselves the wisdom of Jesus so that it becomes us. As a consequence, we naturally transmute and involve this new understanding into our daily lives. In doing so hierarchy is transcended and a radical egalitarianism found.

It is also reminiscent of Dogen's "Circle of the Way in Continuous Practice." This is the continuous practice of discovering one's original nature, and the cyclic and continuous rotation of the elements of practice with no gap. Thomas must come full circle so that what he knows is always and continuously reflected in his actions in the world, not some "other" and more ethereal state of being.

That he has at last done this is indicated in his final dialogue with the other disciples. Like Jesus, he gives his own turning words for them to contemplate. Thomas is now the "teacher." "If I tell you one of the things he said to me, you'll pick up stones and cast them at me, and fire will come out of the stones and burn you up."

He knows better than to reveal the turning words of Jesus, for it would only confuse them. He does not leave them totally bereft, however, since he presents a metaphor for the fire that kills the idea of a teacher and a philosopher. This is the fire of saying 10, the one that Jesus has cast upon the world and is guarding until it blazes. While Peter and Matthew might initially reject that fire by throwing the metaphorical stones of outrage against blasphemy, if they accept the truth of the living Jesus, then it will burn away their delusions.

Case 2 of the *Record of Transmitting the Light* states that when the wisteria has withered, the trees have fallen, and the mountain has completely collapsed, the water in the valley overflows and from the stones fire gushes forth. This is a metaphor for dying to self and the energetic fullness that emerges in its place. The last two disciples must not only taste this water of clear seeing but imbue it with a fiery energy that consumes the separate self and burns away delusions.

17

THE DONKEY AND THE WELL

He said, "Lord, many are gathered around the well, but there's nothing to drink."

—*Gospel of Thomas*, saying 74

Sushan Kuangren once said to a senior monk of his community, "The true Dharma-body of Buddha is like the empty sky. It manifests its form corresponding to things—just like the moon on the water. How do you explain the principle of this corresponding?" The monk said, "It is like a donkey looking into a well." Sushan said, "You put it in a nice way, but you were able to say only eighty percent." The monk asked, "What do you say, master?" Sushan said, "It is like a well looking at a donkey."

—*Book of Equanimity*, case 52

In saying 108 Jesus suggests that whoever drinks from his mouth will become like Jesus. Division and separation will be overcome. Since Jesus is the very fountain of wisdom, to drink from him is also to become wisdom itself. If we stand around the well and don't drink from it, then we remain ignorant, since this is the way we liberate ourselves. It is the draught of the deathless.

This is why to drink from the ultimate is to drink the cure to the dis-ease of life. This cannot be understood just from a superficial and material level. If we look deeply and remember that the living Buddha, like the living Jesus, is another name for that which is omnipresent, then the "birth" of the Buddha gives rise to a particular consciousness.

This state of being is one that enables the sick, hungry, and thirsty to transcend their material woes and to become detached from their cravings through the discovery of the "unseen." The *Vimalakirti Nirdesa Sutra* points out that enlightened people are themselves food and drink for the tired and sick soul. As it says in John 6:55: "My flesh is true food, and my blood is true drink." Since Jesus the Kingdom is in all things, material and spiritual, everything is transformed by drinking from the mouth of the eternal. The result of attaining the Jesus-self is entrance into the whole. No wonder the *Dhammapada* declares "those who drink deeply of the Dharma live happily in every way, having a mind that is serene."

Those who reject this, as saying 74 tells us, are about the well but are not drinking of the eternal. On one level "nothing to drink" is a metaphor for those who suffer from the dry mouth of no wisdom. They mill about the well of Jesus wondering what his words mean. Due to their own delusion, there is nothing that they can see to drink.

These dry-mouthed people milling about the well are the hungry ghosts spoken of in Buddhism, the folkloric metaphors for remnants of the dead afflicted with insatiable desire, hunger, or thirst as a consequence of bad karmic deeds. They are tormented by unfulfilled and insatiable cravings and often depicted as having pinhole mouths that cannot swallow anything.

These are people who in their past life suffered from their own ignorance and could not see that *amrita*—the nectar or "dew of immortality" that was spiritual nourishment—was just a cup away. If they did know, they would've chanted something akin to the "Short Verse for Preventing Disaster": "I take refuge in the many buddhas who have discoursed on the teaching of no-death. Emptiness, drink up all misfortunes. Drink them dry. Flame, burn away all misfortunes. Incinerate them completely." As those around the well could not do this either, the well is entirely empty to them, and the Kingdom far away.

Similarly, unable to accept that the wellspring of eternity was within himself, a student once petulantly said to Zen Master Jingqing Daofu, "There must still be something yet more transcendental." The master said, "Obviously." "What is the transcendental thing?" the student asked. The master replied, "When you drink the water of Mirror Lake in one gulp, then I'll tell you." To drink the entire Kingdom in one gulp can be done, but it requires intention and unification with our Jesus-self. It requires action.

If the disciples were to acquire the wisdom eye and take that one big mouthful, they would come to know that what there is to see is simply that there is nothing to see and no one to see it. It is all the Kingdom. This is the no separate Jesus, disciple, eye, ear, nose, body, and consciousness hinted at in saying 17, the "not finding Jesus" in saying 28, and the "hidden" things that are revealed to a human one in saying 108. This very life here and now is the Kingdom we can drink from, and by doing so seemingly impossible things outside of space and time can be made real.

Case 52, "Sushan's Dharma-Body," of the *Book of Equanimity*, says:

Sushan Kuangren once said to a senior monk of his community, "The true Dharma-body of Buddha is like the empty sky. It manifests its form corresponding to things—just like the moon on the water. How do you explain the principle of this corresponding?" The monk said, "It is like a donkey looking into a well." Sushan said, "You put it in a nice way, but you were able to say only eighty percent." The monk asked, "What do you say, master?" Sushan said, "It is like a well looking at a donkey."

In his first question the master is quoting the *Golden Light Sutra*, which says that just as the moon is reflected in any body of water, so each thing manifests the true Dharma body of the Buddha. He asks the monk to explain this principle, and the monk gives his simile. In a case of Zen irony the monk is saying that the donkey, usually a creature which makes an ass of itself, is in this case showing wisdom—it's just looking at the well.

It looks. Just that—thusness—is the true Dharma body of the Buddha. That's how it manifests its form corresponding to things. The master says that that's pretty good but here's my analogy—"it is like a well looking at a donkey." This is from the viewpoint of emptiness, where there is neither the one seeing nor the one seen. It is the place where neither subject nor object exists. The reality of the emptiness of the well is the emptiness of no-self.

This emptiness of the well of the Kingdom is boundless, flexible, and always open to possibility. It has no limits. It fills the whole world up because it is the whole world. This is why, when asked by a student "What is the Way?" Zen Master Baling Haojian in case 100 of the *Blue Cliff Record* said, "The clearly enlightened man falls in a well." This is considered a set of turning words precisely because to fully see the Kingdom requires nothing but full immersion in the waters of the living Jesus.

This is what Jesus is pointing at in saying 67 when he says that if a person who knows the all still feels some sort of personal deficiency then he is completely deficient. As the Kingdom itself, Jesus is the all and is everywhere. So when a person has fully realized the Kingdom, they know that they have intimacy with everything; they lack nothing. If they feel that they are lacking even one thing, then they are lacking everything. They have not truly awakened.

The surety of *kensho*, an awakening event, brings the security of knowing our true potential and that all manner of resources in the Kingdom are available to us. To know ourselves, saying 67 points out, is the condition of fullness and joy in the world. Psalms 96:11 suggests that a person who has seen the all does not hesitate to call out, "let the heavens be glad, and let the earth rejoice; let the sea roar, and all that fills it." In the Sutta Nipata, the Buddha himself cried out, "My mind is obedient, it is loosed from all bonds, I have trained it these many years; it is quite docile, no evil is left in me; so fall if you will, O rain of the sky."

Sayings 13, 67, and 108 contain warnings against the wilderness of unfulfilled spiritual longing. They continue the theme of Jeremiah 2:13: "For my people have committed two evils: they have forsaken me, the fountain of living water, and dug out cisterns for themselves, cracked cisterns that can hold no water." In this verse the context was the prophet Jeremiah's assertion that Israel did not maintain a living memory of the experience of God's grace in the wilderness.

These sayings remind us that this covenant of the Kingdom is not only still among us but *is* us. This is why the Buddha pointed out that having drunk this Dharma medicine, we will be ageless and beyond death; having developed and seen the truth, we will be quenched, free from craving. Any distance between us and other things is self-created. As Matthew Henry explains in his expansive Bible commentary, we become true members of Christ's body not merely by drinking the sanctified wine, but by drinking into one Spirit. It is internal renovation that maintains our union with Christ and which allows us to see our place in the universe. When we do this it may not be recognized by others, but it nevertheless completely transforms us and is fully worth the effort.

18

DRUNK AND BLIND

Jesus said, "If someone who's blind leads someone else who's blind, both of them fall into a pit."

—*Gospel of Thomas*, saying 34

Making the eye on the forehead blind, one clings to the mark on the scale. Throwing away body and life, one blind person leads many blind people.

—*Gateless Gate*, case 46

Saying 34 continues the theme of drinking, placing it within both the context of spiritual and material thirst. It links the problematic issue of a lack of thirst for realization with a lack of spiritual vision, so that those who cannot see the Kingdom are likened to the visually diminished equivalent of the spiritually developed.

In saying 34 Jesus gives a warning to us: "If someone who's blind leads someone else who's blind, both of them fall into a pit." This has two aspects to it. The first is related to placing faith and trust in someone who does not have the wisdom eye, and perhaps therefore not our best interests at heart. The second is the importance of spiritual sight in the liberation of people from suffering.

The emphasis upon the need for spiritual sight cannot be understated in *Thomas*. Recall saying 5, which asks us to recognize what is in our sight so that which is hidden from us will become plain. To see clearly is the prerequisite for stepping onto the Kingdom Way since without it nothing else can be in focus. Yet, as Jesus stresses, while the folly of spiritual blindness is disastrous, the rewards of wisdom are life-changing. This reward is the Kingdom itself and is available to all.

The difficulty, as I suggested before, is that seeing the whole of reality requires no less than the death of the separate self, which is why it is both paramount and hard to attain deep insight. Indeed, as the Buddha pointed out, the unaffected is hard to see. It is not easy to seek truth, but to see is to have done with owning. To see the Kingdom for what it truly is allows us to become a solitary one. This necessitates recognizing our ignorance and seeking right understanding as its antidote.

Right understanding or view is the understanding of oneself as one really is. It is at the beginning of the path since wisdom is the foundation out of which all liberation grows. In Buddhism right view is the first facet of the noble eightfold path, the Buddhist ethical action plan for how to live a realized life. The eight elements of the path consist of right view, right intention, right speech, right action, right livelihood, right effort, right mindfulness, and right concentration. Each of these elements interlinks with the others to enable clear sight unencumbered by the filter of the self, the ego, opinions, preferences, aversion, and craving. They facilitate the ability to see the world as it really is rather than how we want it to be.

Right view cannot be attained by clinging to our doctrines and perceptions, as the disciples in sayings 6, 14, 27, 53, and 104 aptly demonstrate. The Buddha once spoke of similar men, the Vedic Brahmins, the specialists of religion in his time, who clung to their beliefs as the "only straight path." He criticized their lack of spiritual sight and was especially concerned about the fact that some people teach about realities that they themselves have never seen. That is not only harmful and dishonest but unfruitful. He also pointed out, "For one submerged in mud to pull out another submerged in mud is not possible."

A verse in the *Dhammapada* teaches that each man must direct himself first to what is proper, and only then can he teach others; in this way a wise man will not suffer. This is the lesson Jesus is teaching us in saying 34—we must be careful of spiritual leaders who do not have clear sight, and we too should foster our own wisdom eye before we seek to express our knowledge and influence people. After all, we could be mistaken about what we see and know.

This is the teaching point contained in the famous Buddhist parable, "The Blind Men and the Elephant." In this story some ascetics were seen arguing over doctrine. The Buddha's followers told him about this, and he commented that since they were spiritually blind they were unaware of good or bad, true or false. Hence, they fought often. He then related a parable in which a king once assembled all the congenitally blind people in his kingdom. He brought them an elephant and told them to touch it and provide an explanation of what the creature was like. After doing so, various similes were put forward. An elephant is like a pot, a fan, a plow-share, a plow-pole, a storehouse, a pillar, a mortar, a pestle, and so on. They all ended up in a brawl, each arguing that their version was correct.

In exactly the same way, the Buddha commented, do people—blind and without insight—fight over which version of the truth should dominate. These kinds of people, he warned, dispute among themselves, saying "this doctrine is true, every other is false. Some people who attach themselves to methods of analysis, and perceiving only one side of a case, disagree with one another." In the famous cat-cutting episode of the *Blue Cliff Record*, an entire group of monks were quarreling about a cat of all things. Seeing this, Master Nanquan Puyuan held up the cat and said, "If you can say something, I will not cut it in two." No one in the assembly could bring themselves to say anything. Nanquan cut the cat in two. This can be read as a metaphor for the act of cutting to the heart of the matter, which is what Thomas asks us to do as well.

It is important to note that, as a wise and compassionate person, Jesus, like Nanquan, is not denouncing spiritually undeveloped people. Instead, he sees them as disoriented and confused. They do not know what they are doing. This is a very different viewpoint from seeing someone as intrinsically evil. Ignorance, an impermanent mind state, can be abandoned and rectified by the light of even the smallest bit of knowledge. So even though we may "fall into a pit," Jesus wants us to know that there is still hope in the wisdom of the Kingdom.

He also expresses his opinion that everyone is redeemable in saying 28, although his exasperation clearly shows through. Even though he "took his place" in the world and gave them their very own wisdom master in the flesh, this had no effect upon some of them.

Jesus made his stand here on this earth in this Kingdom and not in some other place. The *Lotus Sutra* makes it clear that this here and now "is a place of the Way." It is *here*, the sutra tells us, that buddhas attain enlightenment, *here* that they turn the Dharma wheel of teaching, and *here* that they enter *parinirvana* (die). These things do not happen in some other realm but here and now in the very place where we stand. Unfortunately, the fact that Jesus was the embodiment of an enlightened consciousness was of no avail for some.

In saying 28 Jesus laments: "I stood in the middle of the world and appeared to them in the flesh. I found them all drunk; I didn't find any of them thirsty. My soul ached for the children of humanity, because they were blind in their hearts and couldn't see. They came into the world empty and plan on leaving the world empty. Meanwhile, they're drunk. When they shake off their wine, then they'll change." Some people are just not spurred on to seek realization until they have really drunk to the bottom of their lives and can go no further down. For others, they seek intoxication with the world in order to alleviate their suffering in some way. This is only a short-term and expedient measure. Despite this, when the shine has worn off many of us still go back for more. This is why Jesus is disturbed by the fact that some people quench their thirst in unhealthy ways. He could find no one with true thirst for enlightenment.

The unfortunate thing is that the people Jesus is describing are satiated only for a time. Since the separate self is an illusion, and we cannot satisfy a fictional entity, nothing material can ever really be completely and permanently fulfilling. The only true fulfillment is to know the deathless of saying 1. So on a surface level this is warning of the dangers of intoxication since through intoxication we commit wrongdoings and make other people intoxicated. In the Sutta Nipata the Buddha advises us to "avoid this seat of wrongdoing, this madness, this folly, delightful to the foolish." On a deeper level, one which Thomas is more comfortable delivering, it is a comment upon the dangers of attachment, craving, neediness, and thirst for whatever satisfies the separate self.

In Zen the term *blind* is used in an ironic sense to mean those who have deep insight, in other words, those who are blind to the dictates of the self and the entanglements of the intellect. If only the blind people leading others into a pit in saying 34 could be this kind of blind. Case 46, "Stepping Forward from the Top of a Pole," of the *Gateless Gate*, states the following: "Making the eye on the forehead blind, one clings to the mark on the scale; Throwing away body and life, one blind person leads many blind people."

The first two lines refer to those who cover their spiritual sight with the scales of conceptualization. They cling to the mark of their intellect. These kinds of people are truly blind to reality. However, as the last two lines inform us, if we can throw away body and life (concepts), we can lead others of like mind. This is a good sense of blindness because it sees no separation at all.

Unfortunately, Jesus knows and sees that most of our actions arise out of the blindness in our hearts. We do not have spiritual sight to fill them up. Instead, we are empty. This is not empty in the sense of the essential or a lack of conceptualization; it is undeveloped insight. If we do not learn to fully see, then we will die like this as well. Out of compassion for our suffering, Jesus's "soul ached for the children of humanity."

Like the Buddha, Jesus also did not leave it at that. Many people might be spiritually blind and expediently satiated, but at some point they will sober up. So rather than leaving them to their own devices he points to the opportunity to approach them when they are feeling remorse or doubt about the wisdom of their short-term choices. Everyone can "shake off their wine" at some point. This is the precise reason for the existence of the *Gospel of Thomas*.

Sayings 28 and 34 simultaneously express exasperation and hope for those of us who fall off the spiritual bandwagon. They warn us of the dangers of intoxication through spiritually and physically unhealthy means and the unquenchable thirst of the self. Yet the promise of *Thomas* is that the wisdom doors are open to anyone who soberly assesses their life and seeks the Kingdom. The observations and promises of *Dhammapada* 334 and 336 run true: "The thirst of a thoughtless man grows like a creeper; he runs from life to life, like a monkey seeking fruit in the forest, but he who overcomes this fierce thirst, difficult to be conquered in this world, sufferings fall off from him, like water drops from a lotus leaf."

19

THE STONES SPEAK WISDOM

Jesus said, "Blessed is the one who came into being before coming into being. If you become my disciples and listen to my message, these stones will become your servants; because there are five trees in paradise which don't change in summer or winter, and their leaves don't fall. Whoever knows them won't taste death."

—*Gospel of Thomas*, saying 19

Become cold ashes and a withered tree and go on. Become the incense burner in an ancient shrine and go on. Become a strip of white silk and go on.

—*Book of Equanimity*, case 96

In saying 19 Jesus continues his efforts to awaken the disciples' minds to the timeless and eternal nature of the Kingdom. He blesses the Kingdom: "Blessed is the one who came into being before coming into being." He then draws his disciples' attention to the world around them to reinforce the point: "If you become my disciples and listen to my message, these stones will become your servants."

When the separation between ourselves and everything else melts away, "everything as Kingdom" could just as easily be "everything as the table" or even something as small and insignificant as "the stone." The eighteenth-century Jodo Shinshu priest Issa Kobayashi once wrote that even the lowly bamboo shoot proclaims to all the world, "I alone am the World-Honored One." The bamboo shoot is "I alone." It is all of the Kingdom, and we are it.

Since everything on this earth manifests essential nature, even a tree can be a teacher, and so can a stone. The stone, like us, manifests the Kingdom because, like us, it is the whole Kingdom in itself.

Thomas completely switches the dead stone of Matthew 7:9 ("what man if his son asks for bread gives him stone?") into a living one. The joy of this can be found in a poem by the thirty-eighth Zen ancestor, Tozan Gohon Daishi: "How marvelous! How marvelous! The preaching of non-sentient beings is miraculous. If you hear it with the ears, it would be impossible to understand it after all; Only when you hear the voice with the eyes will you be able to know it."

Jesus also creates imagery to illustrate the perpetual nature of the Kingdom: "There are five trees in paradise which don't change in summer or winter, and their leaves do not fall. Whoever knows them won't taste death." These five trees are symbols of worldly equanimity, which is said to allow for an evenness of mind, and that comprehends itself in many other Christian virtues such as meekness, gentleness, temperance, charity, contentment, and consistency. It goes further than that, however.

Zen Buddhists might recall case 96 in the *Book of Equanimity*, which gives advice for meditation retreats.

> Become cold ashes and a withered tree and go on. Become the incense burner in an ancient shrine and go on. Become a strip of white silk and go on.

Each of these is an analogy for the way in which a disciple can come to rest in their true nature. The white silk symbolizes a consciousness that is clean and uncluttered, while the cold ashes and a withered tree represent stillness, calmness, and maturity in practice. The smoke from an incense burner rises up and away in all directions, symbolizing not only the letting-go of attachments, but the ubiquitous nature of the true self.

Zen Buddhists might also be reminded of some lines from the *Song of the Jewel Mirror Awareness* that describe what it is like when the one bowing and the one being bowed to recognize each other: "It is like facing a jewel mirror; Form and image behold each other—you are not it: it actually is you. It is like a babe in the world, in five aspects complete."

It is the meeting of the phenomenal world and true self. The way in which the eternal manifests in this world is likened to a newborn baby in five ways—it neither goes nor comes, and it neither arises, stays, nor speaks. This is why in saying 46 Jesus stated that whichever one of the disciples comes to be a child will be acquainted with the Kingdom.

The five aspects here also refer to the five sense consciousnesses. Babies have not yet developed discriminating consciousness, so this means they are complete with five senses but without the crippling effect of conceptualization. They are an analogy for those who have removed their veil of intellection and have clearly seen the ultimate. Symbolically, "in five aspects complete" also signifies what is known as the five Dharma "bodies" or the five vehicles for the development of true wisdom—meditative insight, precepts, wisdom, liberation, and ultimate wisdom derived from liberation. These five trees of Paradise never fail to give us refuge.

Saying 19 points to the fact that whoever knows these five will not taste death. If we restrict ourselves merely to the world of senses, then we die. Knowledge of the Kingdom is knowledge of our basic nature, which is immutable and timeless. It can never die. As we are not only in the Kingdom but are the Kingdom itself, we do not die either. Provided that we let the stones serve us and take shelter under the five trees of Paradise, the deathless will automatically claim us.

20

RESTING IN THE ESSENTIAL

Jesus said, "When you see the one who wasn't born of a woman, fall down on your face and worship that person. That's your Father."

—*Gospel of Thomas*, saying 15

Rikuko said, "Dharma-teacher Nansen said, 'Heaven and earth and I have one and the same root; all things and I are one single body.' How wonderful this is!"

—*Blue Cliff Record*, case 40

Saying 15 involves Jesus drawing a clear line between those who are realized and those who are not. The basis for this judgment is direct knowledge of the ultimate. Jesus describes not only what it is like to fully see the Kingdom but the rewards that come from doing so.

In saying 15 he speaks to the disciples of "the one who wasn't born of a woman" since they can see the physical womb only as the birthplace of humanity. These two different aspects of reality (*not born of* and *born of*) are metaphors for the essential and phenomenal, or the uncreated and the created. The Udana describes the interplay and relationship between the two in this world:

> There is an unborn, unoriginated, uncreated, unformed. Were there not this unborn, unoriginated, uncreated, unformed, there would be no escape from the world of the born, originated, created, formed. Since there is an unborn, unoriginated, uncreated, unformed, therefore is there an escape from the born, originated, created, formed.

This ultimate reality is the Kingdom, the unconditioned, also known as the unborn, the unoriginated, the uncreated, and the uncompounded. It is the ultimate cause of the universe in which all existences find their essential order and significance.

The uncreated is dynamic universal connection unlimited by finite substance. This is why Zen Master Nansen said, "Heaven and earth and I have one and the same root; all things and I are one single body." Everything arises from the sutra of the uncreated and unborn. *Sutra* in this sense is not the written text but the text of the whole universe.

Saying 15 tells us that unless we see the Father (the Kingdom, the unseen) we cannot fully realize that while we may physically come from a woman, we are not born from one either. The only way this can come about is through clear recognition of the Father, another term representing the essential world. As Zen Master Dongshan Liangjie of the ninth century pointed out, it can never be explained to you by means of one born of mother and father. To expect realization to come only by conventional means denies the fact that absolutely everything in the universe, including nonsentients such as the stones in saying 19, expound the eternal because they are the Kingdom itself. Only the entire universe can teach the entire answer.

When we see the essential (the Father), we are no longer limited to the phenomenal (what is born from a woman) because we move into a new life. When realization occurs, we know the Kingdom intimately, deeply, and immediately. Master Wumen Huikai taught that should you be able to clearly realize who "he" (essential nature) is, it would be as if you met your own father at the crossroads: you do not have to ask your own father who he is. Only when we fully see this panoramic picture can we be reborn as an ihidaya, a solitary one.

Jesus tells his disciples that it is this that they must see if they are to become fully realized. Having done this, it is appropriate to bow in respect and recognition. The very act of bowing is the natural response to opening our eyes and seeing the unseen—we cannot do anything other than fall to the ground in astonishment and gratitude.

In the koan literature of Zen Buddhism the resolution of a koan—in other words the attainment of insight into the essential—is often marked by a monk bowing and leaving. In case 11 of the *Gateless Gate*, "Zhaozhou Examines the Hermits," Zen Master Zhaozhou Congshen once said to a wise hermit that he gives freely and takes away freely, he kills and gives life freely, too. After saying this he made a profound bow. His bow was to show respect to the enlightened person he was speaking to but also to reveal that from his encounter he had attained an equal understanding. The wise hermit had given a teaching, and that had enabled Zhaozhou to kill conceptualization and live fully.

It is traditionally believed that bowing surrenders the separate self completely and so fosters the eradication of the three poisons (anger, greed, and delusion). To put two hands together symbolizes the unification of the phenomenal and the essential, the disciple and the Father. To prostrate oneself and worship the Father is to recognize that worshiper and the worshiped are of one nature. From appearances this may seem like the worship of two different entities, but as saying 15 tells us, the act of bowing is to demonstrate that like sees like.

To behold "the one who wasn't born of a woman" is not to look up and visually see something on high, but rather to clearly envisage and to know for certain our true self. This is exactly the purpose of a bow—to reduce any sense of a small, separate self. When we bow, we bow with an awareness of the totality. Since the one who bows and the one being bowed to are not separate, the communication between them is immutable.

This perfection is reflected in saying 18, which speaks of the circle of the Way in which the beginning and the end mutually encompass each other. Thinking only in finite terms, the disciples ask Jesus to tell them when their end will be. They are looking forward to the time of their reward in heaven after they have died. Jesus replies, "Have you discovered the beginning so that you can look for the end? Because the end will be where the beginning is. Blessed is the one who will stand up in the beginning. They'll know the end, and won't taste death."

The disciples are already asking about the ending of things even though they have yet to discover the source of their very own nature. They are thinking purely in logical, linear, and temporal terms. Yet in discovering the Father, Jesus seems to be suggesting that we discover our beginning (which is also the end). When we wake up and see that reality is both the Kingdom (the Father) and the individual, the one and the many all at once, we free ourselves from the constraints of the created— that which is born from a woman. In other words, we free ourselves from life and death.

This is the fruit of seeing the whole of reality, not just a part of it. In recognizing the Father for who he is (the eternal, the beginning and the end), the disciples can root themselves in the ground of reality, their essential self (the beginning). Despite physically dying at some point (they will know the end), they will not experience death because they have become the Kingdom itself.

In these sayings Jesus is saying to the disciples, "Your ancestors may have eaten and still died, but if you eat this bread you will live forever." As it is said in the Udana, what is born dies but whatever is unborn is undying. In this sense there is no beginning and no end to our existence, since that which is not born of a woman is unending and unborn. It is always the eternal now because the Kingdom is located in experience. This is why the question "tell us about our end" can never be more than a one-dimensional understanding.

21

THE SINGLE ONE

Jesus said, "I'll choose you, one out of a thousand and two out of ten thousand, and they'll stand as a single one."

—*Gospel of Thomas*, saying 23

The Path has no byroads; one who stands upon it is solitary and dangerous. In complete freedom you will be able to wield the sword that kills and gives life.

—*Blue Cliff Record*, case 16

Sayings 23 concerns the single or solitary one, a term that was first introduced in saying 16. This is a person who has become a true renunciant. Many sayings in *Thomas* mention this kind of person. Saying 23 states that those chosen by Jesus, who is the Kingdom itself, will "stand as a single one," saying 49 blesses the "solitary and elect," while saying 75 states that only the "solitary" will enter the bridal chamber. It is obvious that the importance of developing a singular state of consciousness cannot be overstated in the *Gospel of Thomas*. These are the only ones who in saying 62 are said to be worthy of Jesus's mysteries.

When we hear the word *renunciant*, what comes to mind is the monastic or mystic who has retreated to a place of solitude far from the crowd. A renunciant is usually considered to be an ascetic who is more often than not celibate and who has rejected the worldly life in favor of "higher" spiritual practices. This is certainly the interpretation favored by both Christianity and Buddhism.

Yet *Thomas* points to something different—the solitary one is not the person who retreats from the world but who lives within it. This quality of "singleness" entails unity of the heart-mind, as in one who lives aligned with wholeness, a state of inner oneness. When we see through the eyes of nonduality, just the seeing itself is enough. What is it that is seeing? The Kingdom itself. So in seeing, there is just seeing, and in hearing, just hearing. Our true nature is not to see but seeing itself. Just that single thing is everything when the separate person has got out of the way.

Wherever such a person goes they operate within this reframed psychological and religious paradigm. So while the Buddha made a distinction between physical and psychological solitude (with the former considered more important), he also pointed out that without the proper frame of mind, seclusion from others is not fruitful anyway.

Shariputra, the chief disciple of the Buddha, once explained in the Majjhima Nikaya that one person might live in a forest devoting themselves to ascetic practices, but might be full of impure thoughts and defilements; another might live in a village or a town, practicing no spiritual discipline, but their mind might be pure. Of these two, the one who lives a pure life in the village or town is definitely far superior to, and greater than, the one who lives in the forest. It is inner wisdom that ensures entrance into the Kingdom.

The *Cula Assapura Sutta* explains the nature of a true recluse: such a person does not depend on outer observances but purification of the mind. A person accomplished in the proper way of a recluse is described as having abandoned "covetousness, corruption, anger, ill will fades, hypocrisy, malice, jealousy, selfishness, craftiness, deceit, evil desires, and wrong views. Wherever one may live, nonattachment is the mark of the true recluse."

It goes further than virtuous actions, however. It is a mind state. Chastity in this new framework does not necessarily mean abstinence from sex but fealty to one's own essential nature. Moreover, purity is not necessarily freedom from contamination but the virtue that arises out of wisdom insight. The correct understanding of reality takes precedence over anything else.

For this reason, true renunciation doesn't mean physically running away from the world or giving up material things, but maintaining a state of nonattachment. In the perfection of wisdom literature, it is noted that living in forests far away from other people is not true seclusion. True seclusion is to be free from the power of likes and dislikes. Outer situational aspects (such as the geographical context) take second place to the development of a heart-mind that sees no separation between anything. As Zen Master Dogen once suggested, whether you live a monastery or in the secular world is irrelevant. Enlightenment depends solely upon whether you have a sincere desire to seek it or not.

In the *Pathama Migajala Sutta* a monk named Migajala asks about the definition of what in Buddhism is called a "lone dweller" or someone who lives alone. The sutra defines it in terms of a mind that is free from sensory attachments. The word *lone* also means "one." So in meditative terms this means oneness of the mind. In the Samyutta Nikaya it is literally defined as "the one who delights in the auspicious oneness."

For obvious reasons, the Kingdom is not open to just anyone. Only those who have fully incorporated the mystery of the essential can open the door to Jesus. This is why in saying 62 Jesus makes sure his disciples understand that mere lip service to religious practice will not get them far. Instead, only those worthy of his mysteries can be told his mysteries. Not just anyone will do; what is required is someone who concretely embodies the singleness of a solitary one.

"Don't let your left hand know what your right hand is doing" refers to how a disciple acts in the world. Similar to the injunction of saying 93, this is asking them not to give what is holy to dogs. In other words, they must be discerning about who they interact and share their knowledge with. It may also refer to the manner in which they conduct themselves. A solitary one does not act from an egocentric framework but rather from a natural and free-flowing sense of the Kingdom. Zen Master Hongzhi Zhengjue once pointed out that killing and giving life, rolling up or unrolling, is our own independent decision. Killing and giving life, rolling up and unrolling refers to using concepts fruitfully or doing away with obstructions to realization as the situation naturally requires.

So to not let your left hand know what your right hand is doing entails acting naturally in a way that does not feed the ego. Singleness involves the opposite of self-seeking and self-deception, the metaphorical domain of the left hand. The right hand, that of nonduality, acts not out of a sense of correctness, but because it is natural to act virtuously. To pay attention to the left hand leaves a person out of the light.

In saying 75 Jesus points out that many are standing by the door, but it is the solitary who will enter the bridal chamber. This description of union as a marriage has often been used in mystical Christianity as a metaphor for the union of Christ and humanity. Matthew 6:6 directs us to enter this singular chamber of the heart and pray to the Father "in secret." The reward is the attainment of true solitude.

This is described in saying 49: "Blessed are those who are one—those who are chosen, because you'll find the kingdom. You've come from there and will return there." Zen Master Hongzhi Zhengjue observed that when you reflect it you become vast, spiritually solitary, and shining. To enter into the bridal chamber is to unify both the individual and the one while retaining our discrete identity. It is to exist within right relationship, to be a "lone dweller." Only by maintaining the essential world as our base or center, and expressing this through the phenomenal, can we enter the bridal chamber of unity and return to the Kingdom.

In saying 75 Jesus is also making clear the fact that it isn't by adopting some sort of outward form that we become a true disciple. The *Dhammapada* tells us that he who is above good and evil, who is chaste, who with knowledge passes through the world—he is the one rightly called a recluse. Just looking the part and going through the motions are not enough. Standing at the door but not opening it will get us nowhere.

This is because ihidaya is not a title but a state of being. The *Cula Assapura Sutta* makes clear that true recluseship is in neither ritual nor appearance, it is not merely wearing the robes of a monastic, it is not attained merely through naked asceticism or dwelling under a tree meditating, and it is not merely standing upright. Majjhima Nikaya 40 agrees with this, stating that we are not a "homeless brother" simply by doing these things. It points out that a person who thinks this is only a man of straw and nothing more.

The *Dhammapada* also stresses that a person does not become a renunciant merely because he or she stands at the door for alms. Rather, as the Buddha himself showed, "a person dwelling alone, withdrawn, diligent, ardent, and resolute, by realizing it for themselves with direct knowledge, in this very life enters and dwells in that unsurpassed goal of the holy life." This is the "homelessness" of the solitary one who has shattered the ridgepole of the house in saying 71.

An ihidaya has also had the solitary experience of kensho, an enlightenment event through which they entered the Kingdom for the first time. This self-realization involves a kind of celibacy, since we cannot share this with someone else. It's a solitary experience in this sense. As case 16 of the *Blue Cliff Record* points out, "The Path has no byroads; one who stands upon it is solitary and dangerous. In complete freedom you will be able to wield the sword that kills and gives life."

It is no wonder, then, that the "lone dweller" strongly contrasts with the "one who lives with a partner" or "a dweller with a partner," which is used in the *Pathama Migajala Sutta* in a moral sense to refer to craving. A person fettered with attachments is said to be a person "living with a companion." When Migajala asks the Buddha for more clarification, he says that even if a lone dweller lives in a village crowded with all sorts of people, he can still be called a lone dweller. The reason for this is that craving used to be his partner but he abandoned it.

While the term *living with a companion* can broadly refer to anyone that a monastic socializes with or any immoral or distracting relationship that hinders the spiritual life of anyone, it can be used to apply positively where a group of people live together for the purpose of solitary meditation. So if we were to apply "singleness" to a community of like-minded aspirants (monastic or otherwise), it would mean that the community stands in unity, as a single organism.

The Buddha described three kinds of community. The first is based on the power, wealth, or authority of great leaders. The second on convenience to the members, so it will continue to exist as long as the members satisfy their conveniences and do not quarrel. The last kind is an organization with good teaching as its center and harmony as its very life. He praised the last kind as best since the members live in one spirit, from which unity of spirit and various kinds of virtue arise. In such an organization harmony, satisfaction, and happiness prevail.

This, as saying 23 tells us, is not a matter of Jesus pointing to a person and saying "I choose you as a solitary one." The mind of unity is not given to a person—it unfolds. A person stands as a single one when they make an effort to touch the essential. Sayings 23, 49, 62, and 75 all vouchsafe for the fact that the ultimate will respond and choose us when we do this. As saying 94 assures us, whoever seeks will find; whoever knocks from inside, it will open to them.

22

The Territory of the Separate Self

Mary said to Jesus, "Whom are your disciples like?" He said, "They're like little children living in a field which isn't theirs. When the owners of the field come, they'll say, 'Give our field back to us.' They'll strip naked in front of them to let them have it and give them their field. So I say that if the owner of the house realizes the bandit is coming, they'll watch out beforehand and won't let the bandit break into the house of their domain and steal their possessions. You, then, watch out for the world! Prepare to defend yourself so that the bandits don't attack you, because what you're expecting will come. May there be a wise person among you! When the fruit ripened, the reaper came quickly, sickle in hand, and harvested it. Anyone who has ears to hear should hear!"

—*Gospel of Thomas*, saying 21

Even though you see all things, you do not attach to them, but, always keeping your own nature pure, cause the six thieves to exit through the six gates.

—*Platform Sutra*, verse 31

Saying 21 continues the theme of seeking and finding, and making the right choice when the situation requires it. It makes the point that unless we have decisive and clear spiritual insight, the separate self will defend its territory at all costs. It also illustrates both a method and an example of how we can cut through our delusions and enter the Kingdom, as well as the pitfalls of not doing so.

This saying has two focal centers—children in a field and advice to those who are listening to Jesus. In the first part Mary says to Jesus, "Whom are your disciples like?" Jesus replies, "They're like little children living in a field which isn't theirs. When the owners of the field come, they'll say, 'Give our field back to us.' They'll strip naked in front of them to let them have it and give them their field."

There are two possible ways to view this section of saying 21. One emphasizes a lack of understanding while the second alludes to enlightenment. In the former, the children are in a field that is not theirs. This is a metaphor for those who cannot rest in the essential. Instead, they are childish and immature in their practice and understanding of the Way. They see only the phenomenal side of things. Like the man in saying 109, they do not know the treasure in their own field and live divided and estranged from their true nature.

These children symbolize those who, when encountering a moment of pure and unadulterated consciousness, cannot or will not react in a way that builds upon that. This means that they do not make the right choices when they glimpse some insight into the Kingdom. The *Dhammapada* states it clearly:

Those who mistake the unessential to be essential and the essential to be unessential, dwelling in wrong thoughts, never arrive at the essential. Those who know the essential to be essential and the unessential to be unessential, dwelling in right thoughts, do arrive at the essential.

When the owners of the field, our true self, come and ask for their field back, this signifies some sort of prompting for recognition from our essential nature. It longs for reconciliation with the small ego-self.

When the essential does show itself, however, in their ignorance the children undress and give back their clothes and the field without a thought. Since their discernment is based on shallow and false criteria, they mistake the unimportant for the important. They judge the world to be completely physical and so, by their own standards, the owners want material wealth, not immaterial. They do not even show wisdom in a worldly sense.

Contrastingly, an alternative reading puts forward the idea that these children are a symbol of the fully realized. Like the little child in saying 4 and saying 46, they are childlike, not childish. They represent the state of unencumbered enlightenment that recognizes the true unitive state of emptiness.

So when the essential shows itself, they respond to it quickly and appropriately. Someone who sees the ripening of their practice is positively disposed toward the experience and reaps the benefit of continuous contemplation. They undress in its presence and divest themselves of the last vestige of the separate self when the opportunity presents itself. Not encumbered by anything, they live in the world in a nonattached manner like the passerby in saying 42. Taking on the robe of liberation mentioned in saying 37, they are naked to the true self. Unity becomes the standard way of being. As saying 46 states, whoever comes to be a child will be acquainted with the Kingdom.

Both types of disciple can benefit from the advice in the second section of this saying, but it is the latter kind who act on it. Their readiness or state of preparedness allows them to participate fully in mystery. This is why Jesus gave them the following kind of practical advice: "If the owner of the house realizes the bandit is coming, they'll watch out beforehand and won't let the bandit break into the house of their domain and steal their possessions. You, then, watch out for the world! Prepare to defend yourself so that the bandits don't attack you, because what you're expecting will come."

The master of the house is our true self, which can correctly perceive the origin, form, and effect of the thieves who want to break into our heart-mind and carry off our goods, in this case to rid us of any trace of realization. The *Eight Realizations of the Bodhisattva Sutra* points out the threat: form is a den of thieves. In this case, form (the quality of solidity, separateness, and definition) relates to the body-mind continuum known as "humans." Due to the fact that we are embodied consciousness, the nature of the Kingdom is such that unless we pay conscious attention to the workings of this form, it can involve suffering and egoism both within and without.

Form can overwhelm us if we are not vigilant and self-controlled. The *Sutra of One Hundred Fables* warns us that, intent upon worldly interests, those who are greedy for a little gain and support break the pure commandments and lose their various merits. It is likened to a thief who snuck into a rich man's house to steal a piece of embroidered satin, which he used to wrap up such objects as worn clothes, rags, and sundry effects. He was laughed at by the wise. This thief is known in Buddhism as *Mara*, any psychological or philosophical view that obstructs liberation.

Mara exemplifies the unskillfulness that arises from the false sense of self and serves as a warning of the dangers of ignorance. It is representative of what happens when we let our world be dominated by sensory gratification. Mara is the kind of psychological and emotional consciousness that is totally ignorant of the true nature of reality and so seeks to obstruct enlightenment. As a demon figure of sorts, in Mahayana Buddhism he is the personification of death and the antithesis of the Buddha. Since realized people are beyond the reach of life and death, Mara is often frustrated by the fact that he is unable to see awakened people. For this reason, Mara is also called the End-maker, the Dark One, or the Binder.

In the Buddhist canon there are many instances in which Mara constantly endeavors to prevent humans from achieving liberation. In the most famous example, he appears before the Buddha in the form of a demon just prior to his enlightenment and over a long period of time makes every effort to frustrate Gotama's efforts.

This demon throws his army against the Buddha—dislike, hunger and thirst, craving, sloth and laziness, fear, restlessness, gains, honor and fame, undeserved reputation, and exalting oneself and disparaging others. None of these work. In a last-ditch effort, he sends his three daughters, Discontent, Delight, and Desire to tempt the Buddha. The Buddha refuses them and eventually attains enlightenment.

In the face of the armies of Mara it is no wonder that Jesus advises his listeners to be vigilant toward the world. Strengthen yourselves, he says, with great energy or the robbers will find a way to get to you, for the trouble you expect will come. It is in the nature of the world that there will always be trouble, but as John 16: 32–33 reminds us, there is a way to overcome the world while still being in the world. Jesus directs them to the inner threat from their own ego and desires.

It is through mindfulness, vigilance, and taking control of the activities of the senses that we can work toward protecting ourselves from the robbers who will find a way to get to us. More important, it is the perception of separate "things" that possess a separate "Kingdom" of their own that is the most dangerous of all. Insight into the emptiness and nondual unity of the Kingdom is the most powerful protection against the den of the thieves.

If you have awakened to wisdom insight, the *Platform Sutra* tells us, even though you see all things you do not attach to them but, always keeping your own nature pure, cause the six thieves to exit through the six gates. The six gates are the organs through which the six senses (eye, ear, nose, tongue, body, and the conscious mind) operate. The six thieves are those adventitious defilements that use the six senses to create bad karma.

Jesus finishes his exhortation to his disciples by saying, "May there be a wise person among you! When the fruit ripened, the reaper came quickly, sickle in hand, and harvested it." The person of understanding fully discerns when the crop has ripened and is ready for harvest. They have developed proper insight and can gather the fruits of discernment. Galatians 5:22–23 tells us that the fruit of full immersion in the Kingdom is the harvest of love, joy, peace, patience, gentleness, goodness, faith, humility, and self-discipline.

It may be that sometimes we have to tolerate Mara's children as necessary evils. It may also be that we have to delay tackling them until we have developed enough insight to see clearly or until we have developed good enough skills to handle them efficiently. It may also be that what might initially seem negative is actually not. Sometimes also, what starts out as something negative naturally transmutes itself into virtue.

What is certain is that when we finally see into our true nature, on the day of the harvest the weeds will be plainly visible and they will be pulled up and burned. This does not mean that we grab a hoe and dig them up. Rather, when we see the nondual nature of the Kingdom, we realize that it can embrace both good and bad elements in their entirety. The contest of tenant and landlord dissolves.

Saying 21 reminds us that without the wisdom that comes from full reconciliation with our true nature, we cannot integrate those things or people that stand in the way of full realization. Wisdom, the clear seeing of reality, is the cure for all ills. "And being but one, she [wisdom] can do all things: and remaining in herself, she makes all things new: and in all ages entering into holy souls, she makes them friends of God, and prophets." (Wisdom of Solomon 7:27).

23

Be Ready before the Robbers Come

Jesus said, "Blessed is the one who knows where the bandits are going to enter. [They can] get up to assemble their defenses and be prepared to defend themselves before they arrive.

—*Gospel of Thomas*, saying 103

A student came to Zen Master Bankei Yotaku and complained: "I have a very bad temper. How can I cure it?" "That sounds interesting, let me see it," said the master. "I can't show it to you right now," replied the student. "Well, when can you show it to me?" asked Master Bankei. "I don't control it, it just comes out at different times," replied the student. "Then," said Master Bankei, "it mustn't be your own true nature. If it were, you could show it to me any time. When you were born you did not have it, and your parents did not give it to you. This you need to understand."

—*The Record of Bankei*

While saying 21 concerns a householder knowing that a "thief" is going to attack, saying 103 describes a man knowing the place where the "bandits" will invade his "house." This saying reinforces the message that a person who knows where the bandits will enter is fortunate because he can mount a defense and be prepared before they arrive. In other words, if we know that the weakest links in our armor are our deeply entrenched and negative habits, then right within them is the place to make our stand.

These brigands are the armies of Mara. Mara, as mentioned earlier, makes use of certain emotions and conceptualizations dependent upon habituated tendencies. In Buddhism these tendencies are called kleshas, adventitious defilements or nonvirtuous inclinations. Kleshas refer to negative psychological tendencies that produce unwholesome actions and thoughts engendering negative karma.

The Buddha observed twenty nonvirtuous psychological states that are unwholesome and that harden into deep-seated proclivities: anger, hostility, irritation, conceit, deceit, flattery, arrogance, malice, jealousy, stinginess, lack of remorse, lack of regret, lack of trust, laziness, insensitivity, apathy, agitation, forgetfulness, incorrect perception, and heedlessness.

This is where the freedom of dependent origination plays an important part in liberation—if we do not want to experience negative conditions, then we have a measure of control over that. Basic Buddhist logic holds that if you remove the cause, the effect goes away, or as Majjhima Nikaya 115 says, when this is present, this happens; when this arises, this arises. When this is not present, this does not happen; when this ceases, this ceases.

This view of cause and effect means that our very happiness or misery is based upon habits of thought, feeling, and action. If we learn to produce wise thoughts, feelings, and reactions, then we pattern the mind for awareness and vice versa. If we make ourselves fertile ground in which the seed of wisdom can germinate, then it will.

Our Zen story for this chapter illustrates this well.

A student came to Zen Master Bankei Yotaku and complained: "I have a very bad temper. How can I cure it?" "That sounds interesting, let me see it," said the master. "I can't show it to you right now," replied the student. "Well, when can you show it to me?" asked Master Bankei. "I don't control it, it just comes out at different times," replied the student. "Then," said Master Bankei, "it mustn't be your own true nature. If it were, you could show it to me any time. When you were born you did not have it, and your parents did not give it to you. This you need to understand."

This story illustrates the fact that no one is permanently doomed to a life of misery because everyone carries the ability (essential nature) to change their karma. Our defilements and proclivities are not fixed because they are constructed and therefore can be deconstructed. Wisdom provides the knowledge that all highs and lows are both impermanent and nonsubstantial—they are not entrenched, solid, and set.

If it were true that our proclivities were entrenched, solid, and set, they could be produced at will, but that usually can't happen. Recognition of their insubstantiality allows a person to ride the waves of the human condition with equanimity and hope. In this way we know where the brigands of klesha will enter, and so we can muster our energies and arm ourselves with directed mindfulness and restraint before they invade our heart-mind.

The end result, saying 32 tells us, is that we build a consciousness that is like a fortified city built on a high mountain, which cannot fall, but neither can it be hidden. The Buddha put it in this way: "Like a well-guarded frontier fort, with defenses within and without, so let a man guard himself."

Luckily, in the Kingdom all is available to the practitioner—both good and evil. Anyone can draw on one and not the other. Since by nature we are the Kingdom—a boundless reality out of which anything can grow—creating good utilizes an ever-present quality, while not producing evil never actualizes any negative potential.

24

Two into One

Jesus saw some little children nursing. He said to his disciples, "These nursing children can be compared to those who enter the kingdom." They said to him, "Then we'll enter the kingdom as little children?" Jesus said to them, "When you make the two into one, and make the inner like the outer and the outer like the inner, and the upper like the lower, and so make the male and the female a single one so that the male won't be male nor the female female; when you make eyes in the place of an eye, a hand in the place of a hand, a foot in the place of a foot, and an image in the place of an image; then you'll enter [the kingdom]."

—*Gospel of Thomas*, saying 22

While women are not "women" in reality, they appear in the form of women. With this in mind, the Buddha said, "In all things, there is neither male nor female."

—*Vimalakirti Nirdesa Sutra*, chapter 7

Saying 22 looks at the disadvantages of division (of all kinds) and the limitations of provisional categories. It encourages a return to wholeness through the development of a nondual consciousness that overcomes all opposites. This is a return to what some Christians might call "the Eden consciousness," a primordial and nondual awareness.

In this saying a list of opposites is given by Jesus that includes two and one, inner and outer, upper and lower, male and female, and conventional and essential images of reality. It puts forward the notion that a solitary one makes use of these binary opposites without letting them define reality.

Jesus suggests that to function properly within the Kingdom everything must be transformed as we move from a myopic view to the Kingdom view. To enter "into" the cosmic body of Christ is to realize there was no outside in the first place. The Kingdom is all there is. Soen Shaku, a Zen master from last century, taught that when we penetrate through the diversity of all these individual phenomena, we encounter everywhere this indwelling body, and in doing so find the unity or sameness of things. Its essence is infinite, but its manifestations are finite and limited.

This is why Jesus questions the disciples point-blank in saying 89— why do you wash the outside of the cup? Don't you realize that whoever made the inside is the same one who made the outside? We can hear this as similar to the verse of chapter 22 of the *Record of Transmitting the Light*, which states: "For the deity of emptiness there is no inside nor outside." In saying 89 however, the wisdom teacher sounds a little exasperated. He wants them to realize that the Kingdom is like an all-pervading light that shines within and without.

Instead, they probably only see the surface intent of Jesus's words— that it is an injunction against placing too much importance on outside, material things and too little on the contemplation of inner wisdom. Yet Jesus persists with his disciples in a manner similar to Huineng, the sixth ancestor of Zen:

Good friends, there is no greatness or smallness in wisdom, but since all beings cherish in themselves confused thoughts, they seek the Buddha by means of external exercises, and are unable to see into their Self-nature. That is why they are known to be people of inferior endowments. Those beings who do not take themselves to external exercises, but reflecting within themselves raise this original Nature all the time to the proper viewing of the Truth, remain always Undefiled by the passions and the innumerable follies; and at that moment they all have an insight into the Truth. It is like the great ocean taking in all the rivers, large and small, and merging them into one body of water—this is seeing into one's own Nature.

We can infer that this is also what Jesus wants his disciples to know—that what he is saying is not about purification of greedy or superficial desires. He is saying that washing the inside and the outside is not only of equal value, but they are one and the same.

When, as saying 22 states, we are able to make two become one, the inside like the outside, the outside like the inside, and the higher like the lower, then we can fully occupy our true self. Zen Master Yuanwu Keqin once said that to see this is to know that there are no mundane things outside of Buddhism, and there is no Buddhism outside of mundane things. To the Kingdom, "inside" and "outside" are illusions.

To dwell forever in the separate self is to remain in phenomenal categories and to deny the wholeness that is our birthright. As I explained previously, after we attain realization we see that the essential (the one) and the relative (the many) are like the two sides of the hand—together they make one thing. The two become one.

A solitary one says, therefore, that "where there are three, they are without God, and where there is only one, I say, I [Jesus] am with him. Lift up the stone, and you will find me there. Split a piece of wood, and I am there" (saying 30). Jesus, the Kingdom, is suchness itself. In Zen Buddhism *suchness* is a quality of reality, the as-is-ness of the moment. Suchness is the way things really are.

If a person sees each thing as completely separate, however, it is possible to see three, four, or a thousand entities designated by the title "god." This kind of limited vision misses the forest for the trees—the many are seen but not the Kingdom. In seeing only the phenomenal, the mind of separation counts everything, including gods, one by one but misses the one. In reality, there is not one, not two. This is the teaching point of saying 30. In reality we are not one separate thing alone but we are not two completely disconnected things either—both separate (individual) and united (the whole) at the same time.

Theragatha 245 makes the observation that "where a man dwells alone, he is as Brahma; where two dwell, they dwell as gods; where three dwell, it is as a village; where there are more, it is a rabble." It is making a similar point. If we cast a Zen eye at this, we can see that when we are a solitary one we are like Brahma, the deva (god) of creation in Hinduism. We are the one. But we are also more than that. When we are as two, both phenomenal and essential working together in full awareness, both dwell as gods together. Both of these possibilities are true to reality. But to further divide and divide slips beyond that; it becomes a rabble of disparate self-based and intellectual constructs.

As the Kingdom, Jesus is both one and two, so when he sees another fully aware person, he not only recognizes a fellow realized person but is also one with them in the Kingdom. In this way saying 30 completely revisions Matthew 18:19–20: "Where two or three are gathered together in my name, there am I in the midst of them." Unlike this passage, saying 30 argues that Jesus's presence is not invoked merely by getting two or three people together, but by the solitary one, the one who truly sees.

Thomas is not necessarily concerned with collaboration of members of the community following Jesus but emphasizes the lack of spatial and time-dependent divisions between disciples and within their own consciousness. The emphasis is not upon recognition or approval of a transcendent god but upon immanence. Only the solitary one with his deep insight can see the real Jesus.

Once a person is able to make two become one, they then take one step further and live an integrated and virtuous life of not one, not two. With new panoramic vision they see both individuality and the Kingdom everywhere. Not only Jesus but they too can rightly say, "Lift up the stone, and you will find me there. Split a piece of wood, and I am there." They see the stone and the Kingdom, the wood and Jesus, or more correctly, the wood-Jesus.

Saying 22 also points out that indivisibility also applies to the higher and the lower. Whether we know it or not we are all fully immersed in the Kingdom; there is no difference between it and us. The implication here is that we all have the potential to realize our true nature. This is why the *Infinite Life Sutra* teaches that all people have this same potential at heart, whether they are people of higher or lower stations in life. Likewise, the *Treatise on the Awakening of the Nature of Mind* points out that while the world sees that there are male and female, rich and poor, the Way does not. In Paul's letter to the Galatians 3:28 he too reminds us that there is "neither Jew nor Greek, there is neither bond nor free, there is neither male nor female: for you are all one in Christ Jesus."

In order to get his point across, Jesus also tackles one of the most ubiquitous and dominant categories of all—gender. You must fully see the Kingdom, he says in saying 22, so that we "make the male and the female a single one so that the male won't be male nor the female female." If we look through the unified eyes of the ultimate, he points out, there is no separate thing we can label male or female.

In the *Treatise on the Two Entrances and Four Practices*, an earnest seeker of the Way once asked Bodhidharma what it meant to say "a male is not a male, a female is not a female." Bodhidharma answered that if you really seek the enlightenment that relies on the Dharma then you can't grasp at the concepts of masculinity and femininity. Ultimately they are not real. This is the recognition that while we might have different (and utilitarian) ideas of gender, these are only provisional in the larger scheme of things.

To call this nondual position the "third gender," as some people have, still carries the weight of categorization. There is no third gender beyond male and female. Instead, what a realized person sees is that there is only one thing beyond all categories—the eternal itself. This is not a category, label, or object since it is timeless and all-pervading. There is nothing outside of it.

So while we do need some sort of expression to explain this new way of living, to still cling to the notions of gender stinks of the smell of enlightenment. Zen Master Eihei Dogen advised to put all of that away. Forget about such things as male and female, he said. When we have delusions, then we have these absolute categories, but when delusions are eliminated, there is no distinction of male and female. Similarly, Jesus makes clear that to become as a child means to become a solitary one. This kind of person makes use of distinctions but sees their ultimate nature beyond division.

In light of this, the Kingdom does not favor one gender over the other. Both male and female are equally qualified to attain enlightenment since they are the actual Kingdom itself. If one gender were unable to see the Kingdom, that would mean that they were outside the Kingdom, which is not an ontological possibility. To limit the wisdom teachings to only men is to deny the very nature of reality.

As the Song Dynasty's Zen Master Dahui Zonggao commented, the Way is an egalitarian Dharma-gate that has only one flavor. It's irrelevant whether a person is male or female, noble or common. He pointed out that just one moment of insight and we are equal to the Buddha. Chapter 20 of the *Record of Transmitting the Light* also tells us that once we enter this Dharma-gate, we will be the same as all buddhas, while chapter 39 says, "From the very beginning it doesn't take any name or form. How could you preach anything 'higher' or 'lower'?" The transformation into a living one entails living from the ground of our own being, which is genderless.

The *Sutra of Sagara the Naga King* describes what it is like to use the Kingdom as our base of operation. In this state of awareness, our organs of perception are not "male" or "female" eyes, ears, nose, mouth, body, and mind. A person who perceives through emptiness is neither male nor female, because emptiness is neither male nor female. So who is the one who perceives through enlightenment? Any person who has become wisdom itself.

Zen Master Qingyuan Weixin once described this cyclical reconstruction process: "Before a person studies Zen, mountains are mountains and waters are waters. After they have insight into the truth mountains are not mountains and waters are not waters. After this when they take one step further and truly reach the abode of rest, mountains are once more mountains and waters are waters."

In other words, at first we usually only see the outer. When we enter a state of unified consciousness, separation dissolves and we see that outer and inner are the Kingdom. Outer is not outer and inner is no longer inner. We then move beyond this and come back down to earth, so to speak, and utilize our knowledge of both the one and the many in a fruitful way.

Saying 22 gives the *Thomas* version of mountains and waters in the form of re-imaging eyes, hands, and feet. "When you make eyes in the place of an eye, a hand in the place of a hand, a foot in the place of a foot, and an image in the place of an image; then you'll enter [the kingdom]." This discussion of individual body parts applies to every individual thing on the planet writ large.

This saying can be likened to the words of the apostle Paul in 1 Corinthians 12:27 when he called Christ's followers to recognize who they truly were: "Now you are the body of Christ, and members individually." We are not just individual body parts that one by one add up to make Jesus's body. Each one of us is that body and each body part is the cosmic Christ.

Saying 22 asks us to recognize that the eternal has hands and eyes and feet. When we walk, it is also the Kingdom walking. When we touch, it is also the Kingdom touching, and when we see, it is also the eyes of the Kingdom that are seeing. The eyes of true wisdom together with the feet of true practice and the hands of truly virtuous action can arise only out of a correct understanding of the world.

25

DON'T DRAW ANOTHER'S BOW

Jesus said, "It's not possible for anyone to mount two horses or stretch two bows, and it's not possible for a servant to follow two leaders, because they'll respect one and despise the other. No one drinks old wine and immediately wants to drink new wine. And new wine isn't put in old wineskins, because they'd burst. Nor is old wine put in new wineskins, because it'd spoil. A new patch of cloth isn't sewn onto an old coat, because it'd tear apart."

—*Gospel of Thomas*, saying 47

Don't draw another's bow;
Don't ride another's horse;
Don't speak of another's faults;
Don't inquire into another's affairs.

—*Gateless Gate*, case 45

Saying 47 outlines the cycle of seeing the conventional, then the essential, and then back to a life that incorporates both. Essentially, it describes how the process of realization reconstructs the meaning and significance of each thing in the universe. As a way of explaining this it points out that no person drinks aged wine and immediately desires to drink new wine. New wine is not poured into aged wineskins and aged wine is not poured into a new wineskin, or it might spoil. A new patch is not sewn onto an older garment, for there would be a tear.

When we see the totality of reality, we act in an appropriate manner that arises out of a new and transformed understanding. Accordingly, we cannot place new wine into aged wineskins, or they might break, and neither do we drink aged wine and immediately desire to drink new wine. *Upaya* (skillful means) requires that we use our wisdom with discretion as the situation requires. Sometimes we are as wise as serpents and as harmless as doves (saying 39).

As stated earlier, a living one is someone who perceives emptiness. Whatever is determined by the separate self is very different from what arises out of this realized and enlightened state. In the latter we are no longer nurtured just by the milk of a mother's breast but by the milk of wisdom. Our parent is no longer just a father or a mother, but the Kingdom itself. This is the standard mode of operation for someone who has entered the Kingdom.

Solitary ones live a middle way that does not make idols out of infallible binary categories but uses them appropriately and wisely. This *middle way*, as the Buddha termed it, is a mode of existence that lies between the unrestrained and restrictive inclinations of life. Extremes prevent us from entering the Kingdom because instead of seeing all things as relational and interdependent, we judge them by where they lie on a continuum between polar opposites.

These opposites are seen as objective realities, and we use them to separate the world into absolutes such as love and hate, virtue and vice, death and life, religion and science, and praise and condemnation. This view cannot bring peace because it runs contrary to the ultimate oneness of all things. The living one's nondual consciousness, however, transcends opposites. This awareness sees both the conventional and the essential and allows for a panoramic understanding of reality.

So while a shallow interpretation of saying 47 suggests that we shouldn't divide our lives between competing interests such as one master versus another, it is in fact a commentary on the nondual nature of the ultimate. Like case 45, "Who Is He?" of the *Gateless Gate*, at first glance it appears that it is dealing with the way in which we are torn when we seek to reconcile opposites.

Don't draw another's bow;
Don't ride another's horse;
Don't speak of another's faults;
Don't inquire into another's affairs.

In one sense this is about curtailing our envy of another person's success and working on our own. It seems to be warning of the dangers of concentrating on someone else to the detriment of our own spiritual development.

A different reading, however, might be that there is no separation in the first place. If the Kingdom is everything, what is it that we lack? Division promotes a sense of greed and acquisition for whatever we perceive as missing. Yet the nature of the Kingdom is such that the business of others is our business and the faults of others our faults. When another person draws their bow, it is we who are drawing it, and when another person rides their horse, it is we who are riding, too.

True insight tells us that the intimacy of the Kingdom allows us to inhabit "the earth and everything in it." Perhaps this is what the disciples realized in Luke 22:35 when Christ asked them, "When I sent you to spread the Word without purse, bag and shoes, did you lack anything? And they said, "Nothing." Consequently, saying 61 emphasizes that the great death (of the separate self) makes way for the true self. If a person is destroyed (the great death), they will be filled with the light of wisdom (great life), but if they are divided, they will be filled with the darkness of ignorance.

Unfortunately, most of the time we live divided within ourselves. Clinging to the separate ego-self and missing or rejecting the Kingdom, we are often ignorant of the need for reconciliation with the ultimate. Yet, the equality of the Kingdom includes but is also beyond division. It can achieve the seemingly impossible—even mountains will move if we want them to. Why will they move? If everything is the Kingdom, then everything is the mountain. When we move, it is the mountain moving, just as when another person rides their horse, it is we who are riding, too (case 45).

So, if two make peace with each other in this one house, they will say to the mountain, "Move away," and it will move away. The house is the Kingdom, and making peace is the reconciliation of the mind of division (saying 48). In the same manner, when you make the two one, you will become the sons of man, and when you say, "Mountain, move away," it will move away (saying 106).

What Jesus is talking about is the wisdom-view of a solitary one. This is not a rational, linear, and logical view. Zen Master Eihei Dogen once reminded his students that when someone with the perspective of the separate self encounters a mountain and when someone with the perspective of one among mountains meets this mountain, how they think of it or how they see it will be vastly different.

Like Anguttara Nikaya 6:24, saying 106 tells us that a person who is one with the ground of being can split asunder the Himalayan mountains. The *Lotus Sutra* declares that if this kind of person, after grasping Mount Sumeru in the fist, were to hurl it a huge distance, it would be nothing very difficult. Nor would it be so very difficult to shake this whole universe with our hands and throw it away. The possibilities of emptiness mean that we can move the mountain by moving ourselves to the next room. This is what such koans as "Make Mount Fuji Take Three Steps" or "Put Out the Fire a Thousand Miles Away" ask us to do.

No longer bound by the binary framework of ignorance, every one of us, the "sons of man" (and not just the "son of man," a traditional eschatological title applied only to Jesus), can break free of our physical limitations when we want. While these things are considered easier for a solitary one who knows the two truths (phenomenal and essential), it is far harder for those who live divided in the darkness. It is to these people that the words of sayings 47, 48, and 106 are directed.

26

LOVE AND JUDGMENT

Jesus said, "Love your brother and your sister as your very own being. Protect them as you would the pupil of your own eye."
—*Gospel of Thomas*, saying 25

Yangshan Huiji asked Sansheng Huiran, "What is your name?" Sansheng said, "Huiran." Yangshan said, "Huiji, that's me." Sansheng said, "My name is Huiji." Yangshan laughed loudly.
—*Blue Cliff Record*, case 68

Saying 25 suggests that love of self and love of neighbor are mutually inclusive. We cannot have one without the other. This means that in order to live a full life we must love each other as we love ourselves and that to take care of ourselves is to take care of others. This has serious and widespread ramifications for individuals and the wider community.

Various kinds of love are spoken of in Buddhist texts, including warm regard, closeness, worldly love, loving commitment, loving-kindness, affection, and devoted love. Love is considered to have particular characteristics, mainly that of devotion to others' welfare. It is particularly effective for counteracting anger. Love is the state of having a tender mind and is synonymous with tender care. Similarly, compassion, its close neighbor, has the characteristic of devotion to removing others' suffering and is particularly effective for counteracting harmfulness.

Love is exemplified by the wish that all sentient beings without exception be happy, while compassion is the corresponding wish that they be free from suffering. Unsurprisingly, the Buddha praised even the smallest demonstration of loving-kindness, saying to his monks in the *Culacchara Sutta* that anyone who maintains a loving mind even for just the duration of a snap of fingers can be considered a true recluse.

The Buddha, like Jesus, came into the world out of sympathy for humanity. His prime motivation was the welfare of others. Enlightened people, he pointed out in the Majjhima Nikaya, have always been in the world to aid and assist us. "A nondeluded man," he said, "is born in the world for the good and welfare of many, born out of compassion for the world and for the welfare of men."

In the *Lotus Sutra* he reassured his followers that all the tathagatas (buddhas) in times past existed in countless, innumerable spheres in all directions for the weal of many, the happiness of many, out of pity to the world, for the benefit, weal, and happiness of the great body of creatures. We should not only emulate these people as much as possible, he instructed, but become them. In establishing monastic communities in the world, the Buddha revealed his wish that his message must continue well into the future.

The continuance of a religious practice necessitates certain ways of acting and seeing that build up rather than tear down unity. Mutually beneficial love is one such thing, the Sutta Nipata reminds us, "since those who love all beings have no enmity for anyone." Indeed, the *Dhammapada* tells us that hatred does not end by hatred at any time: hatred ceases by love; this is an old rule. In saying 25 Jesus urges his disciples to do precisely this—to love one another not just for their own sakes but for the good of all. "Love your brother and your sister as your very own being. Protect them as you would the pupil of your own eye," he says.

In a like manner, in the *Kakacupama Sutta* the Buddha taught his disciples the following vow about the necessity of a loving mind:

> May our minds not become corrupt. We will not utter evil speech. We will continue to have sympathy for the other individual's welfare. We will have loving minds and be free from anger. We will continue to relate to that individual who had addressed us with love in our minds. Making the entire world the object of our minds endowed with love, we will continue to relate to the entire world with minds endowed with love—that are untroubled, free from enmity, vast, enlarged, and measureless.

Love kept to oneself and only those we hold dear is limited and can descend into selfish and preferential affection.

So whatever love a person develops they should not keep it just for their immediate loved ones but extend it to all. The Buddha advised that, as a mother protects her only son even at the risk of her own life, so we too should cultivate love without measure toward all beings. He urged us to cultivate toward the whole world—above, below, around— a heart of love, unstinted, unmixed with the sense of differing or opposing interests.

The Buddha, like Jesus in saying 25, also drew a direct correlation between an individual's development of wisdom and the welfare of others. He taught that whoever protects himself protects others by sustaining meditation, cultivating it, and practicing it frequently. Conversely, the Samyutta Nikaya points out that we protect others by protecting ourselves through patience, harmlessness, love, and tender care. In other words, if a person takes care of their own heart-mind, they can protect both themselves and others by means of love.

In saying 25 Jesus asks his disciples to love one another "as your very own being." Love of self is love of other. A totally aware person can love their brother and guard him because their own love is fully developed.

This saying argues that we must develop our own insight before we can help others.

Developing insight cannot happen if we are busy judging each other. This is why saying 26 specifically zeroes in on the lack of virtue in hypocrisy and judgmentalism: "You see the speck that's in your brother's eye, but you don't see the beam in your own eye. When you get the beam out of your own eye, then you'll be able to see clearly to get the speck out of your brother's eye." As Udanavarga 252 points out:

> It is easier to see the faults of others than those of oneself; the faults of others are easily seen, for they are sifted like chaff, but one's own faults are difficult to see. It is like the cheat who shows the dice of his adversary and hides his own, calling attention to the shortcomings of the other player, and continually thinking of accusing him; he is far from seeing what is right dharma, and greatly increases his unhappy lot.

For this reason, the Buddha instructed his followers not to judge others since those who judge others only harm themselves. What appear to be faults in others may actually be reflections of our own emotional afflictions rather than theirs. The *Dhammapada* tells us not to look at the faults of others or what others have done or not done; just observe what we have done and not done.

In case 35 of the *Blue Cliff Record* Manjushri asked Mujaku, "Where have you come from?" Mujaku said, "From the south." Manjushri said, "How is the Buddhist Dharma in the south maintained?" Mujaku said, "The monks of this age of the perishing Dharma are venerating the precepts a little." Manjushri said, "How many monks are over there?" Mujaku said, "Three hundred here, five hundred there." Mujaku asked Manjushri, "How is the Buddhist Dharma maintained here?" Manjushri said, "Worldly beings and saints live together, dragons and snakes are mixed with each other."

The first question is a sassho, a checking question. It is asking whether Mujaku thinks he comes from just one place or whether he knows he is every place in the Kingdom. Mujaku replies that the monks are generally unethical. This answer shows that he is not realized because his first instinct is to judge. Mujaku then asks a question seeking a similar type of response from Manjushri since he is asking about the standard of monastics. Again, he has revealed his mind state. Manjushri seems disconcerted at this judgmentalism so he prevaricates, saying, "A few here, a few there." He doesn't fall into the trap of putting someone in a box or of seeing only the phenomenal.

Mujaku's question, "How is the Buddhist Dharma maintained here?" brings him a little closer to where he should be. Manjushri, in his compassion, answers, "Worldly beings and saints live together, dragons and snakes are mixed with each other." He is trying to point out to Mujaku that although there are ethical and unethical people, all things are within the Way. In the ultimate are male and female, saints and sinners, old and young, healthy and ill. Regardless of how we feel about people, they are emptiness nonetheless. This is why Jesus asks us to love our neighbor and not *like* them because *like* can be fickle and biased. It separates. Unconditional love, however, places no demands on the Kingdom at all because that is its very nature.

Before Mujaku can evaluate others in a fitting manner, he has to see the whole of reality, because otherwise he is just positioning himself higher than others. After all, it is possible to make a judgment without involving the lenses of ego. In the *Dhammapada*, the Buddha made a distinction between an unjust person who decides things in a hasty, forceful way, and those who distinguish both right and wrong, who are well-schooled in their spiritual tradition and lead others not by force but by the Dharma and equity. This sort of person he called *just*. So to pass judgment doesn't always mean you're judgmental in the sense of being unreasonable, irrational, arbitrary, or condemning. If one speaks out of a truly realized state, then that is an entirely different base from which to operate.

The reason for this is clear—judging others out of a sense of self prevents us from fully inhabiting the Kingdom, our essential nature, and only increases those things that build up a barrier of separation. The *Platform Sutra* states plainly that if we see the errors of others then it only increases our own errors. It urges us to eliminate any inclination to see faults. Aversion and attraction have nothing to do with the eternal, it tells us, so stretch out both legs and lie down.

To "lie down" is to rest in the repose of the perfect rest mentioned in saying 2. It can be achieved only by removing "the beam out of our own eye" first and only then helping others to do the same. To remove this beam is to do away with the ego-based separate self that is the cause of dissension and conflict.

Enlightened people know that no one can save another; it is up to each person to see the hidden for themselves. As the *Dhammapada* points out, a wise person knows that by oneself is evil done and by oneself we are defiled. By oneself is evil left undone; by oneself is one made pure. Purity and impurity depend on ourselves; no one can purify another. The Jesus-self is everything, and it is this that heals divisions and restores health. This is contingent, however, on our own effort to bring it out into the open. This is our part of the bargain.

Hypocrisy however, is a form of klesha, the weapon of Mara. Majjhima Nikaya 7–8 tells us that "knowing hypocrisy as a defilement of the mind, a wise person dispels it, saying to themselves, 'Others will be hypocritical, we will be free from hypocrisy.'" For hypocrisy, the alternative is nonhypocrisy. A person who has dispelled hypocrisy, the Buddha said, as well as letting go of anger, hatred, and pride, can truly live the holy life. It is this alternative way of being that Jesus wishes his disciples to foster.

Jesus is also drawing a direct link between the development of love in an individual and the state of one's community as a whole. In the *Cakkavatti-Sihanada Sutta* the Buddha tells the story of how a lack of love and compassion in a particular kingdom directly led to community disaster and social upheaval. The sutras tell us that we arise out of love, that the universe is great compassion itself. To go against this is to go against reality. Dissension and conflict are bound to ensue.

This is why aversion and hatred oppose the reality of the Kingdom, because they are based on ideas of a separate, permanent self. This is a delusion and why, similar to Matthew 7:12, the golden rule in Buddhism is to consider others as ourselves. It is wise, the Sutta Nipata tells us, to always think: "As am I so are others, as are others so am I; harm none nor have them harmed." An old version of the *Dhammapada* contains the biblical-like injunction to "remember that you are like unto them."

In case 68, "Yangshan's What's Your Name?" of the *Blue Cliff Record*, "Yangshan Huiji asked Sansheng Huiran, 'What is your name?' Sansheng said, 'Huiran.' Yangshan said, 'Huiji, That's me.' Sansheng said, 'My name is Huiji.' Yangshan laughed loudly. These two adepts are on the same level of insight and just enjoying themselves and the intimacy of emptiness. They know that we need labels to relate to things but in the end even the label "essential world" is empty. We all carry everyone's name.

Accordingly, to lessen other people's suffering is to lessen our own. The *Vimalakirti Nirdesa Sutra* tells us that the Buddha said, "Your suffering is my suffering and your happiness is my happiness." He urged us not to forget that spirit even for a single moment because it is the nature of buddhahood to be compassionate. So in asking his disciples to love one another Jesus is not asking them just to be nice; he is asking them to act from their essential nature. He knows that enlightenment and morality are one. Due to the very nature of the Kingdom you cannot have one without the other.

Throughout *Thomas* Jesus shows that he identifies himself with the suffering and the ignorant. He is free from religious attachment and moralistic judgment and from the dualities of the world. He has both worldly knowledge and spiritual wisdom. He never grows tired of his efforts to help his disciples awaken, nor does he ever hesitate to help them. In every single one of the 114 sayings he demonstrates a completely unconditional, altruistic, nondual love. Put simply, he is a bodhisattva. In Zen a bodhisattva is a person who devotes themselves to the welfare of others.

In fact, sayings 25 and 26 could easily operate in the same koanlike manner as Zen bodhisattva precepts do. The bodhisattva precepts are a set of guidelines for ethical conduct taken from a Mahayana text known as the *Brahma Net Sutra*. These are not commandments as such, and they do not come with stringent repercussions for code violation. The precepts are not intended to be taken as absolutes.

Much in the same way Jesus recommends we fast and pray in sayings 14 and 27, they are to be held in a flexible yet intentional manner and without attachment to purity or impurity. In teaching the precepts Shunryu Suzuki Roshi pointed out that if we understand the precepts literally then it violates the fifth precept: "Don't be intoxicated." Even the teaching is like wine if we stick to it and are intoxicated by it. For Zen Buddhists, the precepts are not a way to attain something special such as powers of concentration. Instead, they allow us to act freely from our essential nature.

In my lineage, the Harada-Yasutani line of Zen, there are sixteen bodhisattva precepts, two of which are specifically relevant to a discussion of sayings 25 and 26. While Jesus speaks of hypocrisy and love, these two bodhisattva precepts focus on not speaking of others' errors and faults, and not elevating ourselves and blaming others.

Like sayings 25 and 26, these are not just about following rules or being fair and ethical. Nor are they purely about cultivating and encouraging respectful speech and action. They are expressions of ultimate reality itself. If we take not speaking of others' errors and faults, for example, it means that we work out of the realization that our original nature is pure and bright, and this is the same for everyone else. To slander another person is to buy into a world built on distinction between self and other. It creates pain and divisiveness.

We also work intentionally with whatever the eternal now is offering us, and we accept responsibility for how we respond to that. As long as we focus on others, we avoid working on our own faults, but to take a good long look at ourselves is really the mark of someone who is on a spiritual path.

As for not elevating ourselves and blaming others, this focuses on cultivating and encouraging both self and other to abide in our awakened nature. While it is certainly tempting at times to praise ourselves, it arises out of a misunderstanding of the interdependent nature of self. If we truly see that self and other are one, it does not make sense to defend ourselves as superior beings. There may be times when we feel we must criticize others, but if we work with an understanding of essential nature, we can be aware of motive and intent.

Sometimes both the prohibitory aspects of Zen precepts and the encouraging aspects are expressed together. So, for example, the precept "Do not speak of others errors and faults" may be counterbalanced with something like "Accept the moment," "Overcome my own shortcomings," or "Realize self and other as one." In this way abstention and action are contained within one precept. If we apply this to *Thomas*, it would be expressed this way: "Do not be hypocritical and judge others: Love your brother and your sister as your very own being." Alternatively, it might also be: "Provide no shelter for the judgment of the separate self: Giving refuge to others as you would the pupil of your own eye is to see the Kingdom."

The social ramifications of an inability to love and guard our brothers and sisters are immense. The Udana draws attention to an objective fact: "Look where you will, there is nothing dearer to man than himself; therefore, as it is the same thing that is dear to you and to others, don't hurt others with what pains yourself." In order to do this the Buddha urged his followers to specifically cultivate the sublime attitudes of universal love, compassion, sympathetic joy, and equanimity. Love (also translated as loving-kindness) is the first part of the four divine conditions of abiding (in virtue), the other three of which are compassion, sympathetic joy, and equanimity.

Also called the four immeasurables, these are considered four qualities of love, that is, four qualities of the Kingdom. These divine states are called immeasurable because their effects and nature are endless, and they are also called divine abodes because they allow us to abide or rest in a loving state of being. The Buddha stressed that these divine states are not merely finite attitudes that we develop along the way. They are reality itself, and they arise out of the great emptiness.

The deeper meaning of saying 25, then, is that love and wisdom are synonymous with each other. Love is the natural outcome of seeing the interrelational nature of reality. In ignorance we foster partiality and attachment to our own emotions and insecurities. The end result is an artificiality of division between those we favor and those we don't. The true and essential nature of the Kingdom, however, is the equality and unity of all sentient beings.

Recognition that love and wisdom are synonymous finds its expression and fruition in compassion for others. D. T. Suzuki had this to say on the subject:

The questions: "Why have we to love our neighbors as ourselves? Why have we to do to others all things whatsoever we would that they should do to us?" are answered thus by Buddhists: "It is because we are all one in the dharmakaya, because when the clouds of ignorance and egoism are totally dispersed, the light of universal love and intelligence cannot help but shine in all its glory. And, enveloped in this glory, we do not see any enemy, nor neighbor, we are not even conscious of whether we are one in the dharmakaya. There is no 'my will' here, but only 'thy will,' the will of dharmakaya, in which we live and move and have our being."

The irony of sayings 25 and 26 is that, in pointing out to his disciples that they are busy judging others while missing their own judgmental mind, Jesus is asking them to discover the nature of reality. That is, since in the Kingdom there is no separation, on an ultimate level the "speck in your brother's eye" is also "the beam in your own eye."

Separation between ourselves and others is just a delusion; other people are the Kingdom, too. The deeper meaning of saying 25 and 26 is that loving others is to love ourselves, and loving ourselves is to love others. This is not just because it is a compassionate thing to do but because it is the true nature of reality.

27

CHILD OF A GOOD FAMILY

"Whoever doesn't hate their [father] and mother as I do can't become my [disciple], and whoever [doesn't] love their [father] and mother as I do can't become my [disciple]. For my mother [. . .], but [my] true [Mother] gave me Life."
—*Gospel of Thomas*, saying 101

One's father and mother are truly not one's "parents" and the Buddhas are not the "Way"; if you wish to know that which is genuinely closest to you, it is not something to be compared with a father or mother.
—*Record of Transmitting the Light*, chapter 10

Saying 101 pushes us into an understanding of the wider parental role of the eternal. It shocks and comforts us by suggesting we reorient our view of familial ties to include a much bigger father and mother— our essential nature. In doing this, we are called to step out of our conceptual boxes and take up our own cross of understanding in the exact same way that Jesus did in saying 55.

Thomas sets the scene to saying 101 with saying 99 as a precursor. In this saying Jesus's disciples draw attention to the fact that his mother and father are standing outside. As a clever teacher, Jesus sees this as an opportunity to help awaken the disciples. So instead of asking his parents to come in, he tells the disciples that whoever is in sync with the father, the essential world, is his family. We can imagine that the disciples might have been completely silent when they heard that, rolling the implied meaning around and around in their heads. You can practically hear them thinking what does *that* mean? This is a koan worth sitting with for a long time.

It is easy to assume here that Jesus is talking about renouncing familial ties in order to enter the monastic life. True to form, *Thomas* requires us to go beyond renouncing family and to savor and feel the saying to find its deeper meaning, the one Jesus really wants us to find. In essence, he is asking them his own version of case 23 of the *Blue Cliff Record*, "Show me your original face, the face you had before your parents were born."

Saying 101 is not requiring a rational answer such as the definition of cause and effect in dependent origination. It is not seeking genetic ancestry or something located at a fixed point in time and space. It is asking the disciples to see with the eye of nonconceptual, nondualistic wisdom—the re-imaged eye mentioned in saying 22. This is knowing with every fiber of your being the radiant light of saying 24.

Our original face is not an object or a thing but everything (and nothing). This is why we cannot become aware of it except in terms of what we see in front of our face (saying 5). Whoever does the will of the father who is our original face fully rests in their essential nature and operates out of that. That's obeying the natural order of things and is the one common family of every human being on this planet.

The importance of having an open and receptive consciousness such as this is reflected is the many phrases used in Buddhism that include the word *child*. To put on monastic robes in order to embody the Way is to become "a child of Buddha." In some sutras, the Buddha addressed individual disciples as "child of a good family" with *family* meaning the community of truth seekers. To be a child of the Dharma is to be in a continuous state of learning and of refining our own understanding. It is to be "the elect of the father" (saying 50). Without this knowledge, the disciples will be weighed down by conventional categories and only partially informed of the truth. They must become children of the father.

The metaphor of all devotees and practitioners as Buddha's "children" is common in Buddhism, while the use of personification to represent the dharmakaya also features in some sutras. The function of this "father," known in Mahayana Buddhism as the "sole cause" for buddhas to come into the world, is to enable each and every person to become enlightened. The compassionate father rescues his children (all sentient beings) from the burning house of ignorance. This is described in the *Lotus Sutra*:

> He, the Tathagata, endowed with Buddha-knowledge . . . is the father of the world, who has reached the highest perfection in the knowledge of skillful means, who is most merciful, long-suffering, benevolent, compassionate. He appears in this triple world . . . in order to rouse people to supreme and perfect enlightenment . . . He says, 'Verily, I am the father of these beings; I must save them from this mass of evil . . . I, the great Seer, am the protector and father of all beings, and all creatures who, childlike, are captivated by the pleasures of the triple world, are my sons.'

In the *Diamond Sutra* one of the Buddha's disciples, Subhuti, comes to him with a question to be answered for the assembled crowd. Subhuti asks, "How should the son or the daughter of a good family, after having entered on the path of the Bodhisattvas, behave, how should he advance, and how should he restrain his thoughts?" He wants to know how we should follow the Way, keep our thoughts under control and the mind directed to awakening.

The Buddha tells him that he should always keep in mind that we practice the Way not just for ourselves but for others, too. So we should always be thinking how to help others discover their inner light. Their light is our light and vice versa. We are all children of the eternal because we are the eternal. Judging by sayings 53, 101, and 103, however, the disciples don't understand this. They obviously didn't understand what Jesus was initially saying, and so he had to resort to direct and shocking methods to jar them out of their usual ways of seeing the world.

In Zen, teachers employ a great variety of methods to shake the foundation of our entrenched beliefs. These include puns, witticisms, non sequiturs, paradoxes, irony, jokes, even iconoclastic irreverence toward sacred figures and texts. In a similar manner, in saying 105 Jesus takes to calling deluded people "bastards," and in sayings 53 and 101 he calls upon the disciples to "hate" their parents and to "not love" them.

This is not to be taken literally. To enable his disciples to see as he does, he must use drastic strategies to unhinge them from the beliefs of the self. This does not mean, as I explain later, that he is calling for rejection and abhorrence of anything remotely related to family. Rather, he is trying to rattle the separate self into fleeing, much the same as Zen masters of old did when they struck a student or suddenly shouted at them.

When we read *Thomas*, we must remember that Jesus is often talking from the point of the eternal, and not the conventional wisdom of the world. He is aware of things most people aren't. With this in mind we can see that the most important words in sayings 55 and 101 are "as I do" (sometimes translated as "in my way"). Jesus is calling upon the disciples to see things in the way he does—with the wisdom eye. To call upon people to "hate their [father] and mother as I do" is not to actually reject and deny our mother and father, but to deny the limiting conception of them as "mother" and "father." This is what Jesus "hates."

Chapter 9 of the *Record of Transmitting the Light* points out that our father and mother are truly not our "parents" and the Buddhas are not the "Way"; if we wish to know that which is genuinely closest to us, it is not something to be compared with a father or mother. We can read this as saying that in whatever manner we conceive of the Way and of our parents, they are more than that because they are the Kingdom.

It appears that what the world thinks is a "parent" Jesus considers shortsighted. Our parent is also the Kingdom that gave birth to all of us. This does not mean, as some would expect, that we automatically renounce our genetic heritage and all the love and caring we have received from family members throughout our lives. It is, in fact, paying a compliment to our parents.

This is because the Kingdom includes our birth parents but it is also more than them. As saying 101 intimates, Jesus's mother, Mary, physically gave birth to him but his true mother gave him life. His true mother is wisdom itself. All virtues are encapsulated within wisdom. It is only wisdom that finally and completely eradicates ignorance. This is how he came to truly live.

For this reason, in Mahayana sacred texts, wisdom is sometimes referred to as the "great mother of all buddhas." It is given a feminine epithet because, as with "queen of all buddhas," transcendental wisdom gives birth to and raises buddhas and bodhisattvas. The *Prajna Paramita Sutra on the Buddha-Mother's Producing the Three Dharma Treasures* outlines why Buddhists emphasize the recollection of mother wisdom—that to reject the mother (the perfection of wisdom) is to wander in the ocean of birth-and-death forever. To be blind to wisdom is to see through the eyes of our own ignorance and nothing more.

Both the phenomenal and the essential are needed for life to occur. As such, there is no rejection but inclusion, as our parents are now seen as ourselves. This is an even greater intimacy with them than ever before. The only thing that has died is the intellectual box we have placed them and ourselves in. To "hate" is to set aside limited conceptualizations and philosophies and to be dispassionate toward a world built around the separate self. If we do not "take up the cross" of true wisdom, we cannot ever hope to be a true disciple of the living Jesus.

To know only the phenomenal side and to see intimacy only with blood relatives is to reject the true self. Blood may be thicker than water, but so is the love of the Kingdom. Both are true at the same time. So as sexist and crass as it may be, the phrase "bastard" (sometimes translated as "son of a harlot") is nonetheless attempting to describe a person who is the offspring of one tied to the sense gratification and the physicalities of the world. The father and mother in these sayings are birth parents and not the Kingdom as father and mother. Knowing only this kind of existence is to deny the paternity and maternity of emptiness. It is not a literal insult regarding someone's heritage or sexual behavior.

We can see this in a similar text in the Udanavarga, which says:

He who has killed father and mother and two kings, and who has killed an irresistible tiger, is without sin, is a Brahmana [a holy person]. Having killed father and mother and two kings, having conquered their kingdoms with their inhabitants, a man will be pure.

This is not an injunction to be violent. Sometimes when we hear Zen sayings such as "If you meet the Buddha, kill the Buddha" (*Gateless Gate*, case 1) or stories about cats being cut in two (*Gateless Gate*, case 14), it can seem that Buddhism condones some pretty violent acts. Like saying 55 and 101, however, these are not intended to be literal but to hit us with a metaphorical slap.

In the above verse the mother represents craving and the father self-conceit. The two slain warrior-kings are the extremes of eternalism and nihilism, while the kingdom that has been conquered is sense organs and sense objects. Its inhabitants are feeling and perception, because they are the foremost and principal members of the six internal senses. The verse also suggests eradicating a tiger. The commentary on this states that "as the tiger in its natural ferocity devours unhesitatingly flesh and blood, so likewise, he whose mind is bent on evil or spitefulness devours all the roots of virtue."

Together these five things are symbolic of the five mental hindrances to enlightenment—sensory desire; ill will; sloth, torpor, or drowsiness; restlessness or worry; and uncertainty or skepticism. These all distract a person from the path and increase unwholesome states of mind. To not give them life is to "kill" them.

All of this does not mean that the Buddha and Jesus denigrated familiarity and intimacy between people. As I said, the Kingdom includes all of this, too. So while both Buddha and Jesus asked their followers to renounce family ties in order to enter the monastic order, they did not leave them without familial comfort.

Having recognized that the community could not properly function without good companions on the Way, the Buddha declared in the *Itivuttaka* that though the monks were not his genetic offspring, nevertheless they were his true sons and spiritual heirs. In other words, they were family united in Dharma. As Zen Master Guishan Lingyou once observed, as we tread the path it is essential to have good companions. We should listen to what they have to say and put it into practice. This is how we can say that it was our parents who gave birth to us but it was our companions who raised us.

Sayings 55, 99, 101, and 105 tell us that we are nurtured not only by the milk of our parents' kindness, but the universe's as well. Whenever we feel isolated or without support, we would do well to remind ourselves that everyone and everything in the universe is our brother and sister. This may not immediately rid us of a sense of deficiency, but it certainly puts us on the path toward establishing connection and intimacy with the world.

28

MOVEMENT AND REPOSE

Jesus said, "If they ask you, 'Where do you come from?' tell them, 'We've come from the light, the place where light came into being by itself, [established] itself, and appeared in their image.' If they ask you, 'Is it you?' then say, 'We are its children, and we're chosen by our living Father.' If they ask you, 'What's the sign of your Father in you?' then say, 'It's movement and rest.'"

—Gospel of Thomas, saying 50

The solitary light, exquisitely radiant, never darkens itself. As the wish-fulfilling pearl, as the priceless gem—it shines in various ways.

—Record of Transmitting the Light, chapter 14

Saying 50 is based on the idea that to find the Kingdom we have to find ourselves, and this requires making manifest our true image or nature. Either we discover this and reap the rewards (movement and rest) or we remain in ignorance, unaware of the primordial wisdom light. In saying 77, Jesus says, "I am the light shining upon all things. I am the sum of everything." This is the crux of sayings 50, 77, and 101—we are ourselves the light of the Kingdom. This automatically means that when we know this we also discover everything else is as well.

In Buddhist texts those who are awakened are often described in terms of light. The Buddha's own son, Rahula, described him as the "Torchbearer of Humanity." Sir Edwin Arnold who wrote about the life and teaching of the Buddha in verse, called him "The Light of Asia." In the Sutta Nipata it is written that there is only one who abides dispelling darkness, that is the high-born, the "luminous Gotama of great understanding, Gotama of great wisdom."

The *Buddhacharita* describes the light of Buddha as "incomparable," of "infinite splendor" and "infinite brilliance." The *Pajjota Sutta* lists the Buddha as one of the four kinds of light in addition to the moon, the sun, and fire. Like the moon he is reflected in all things, like a fire he has burned away delusions, and like the sun he shines his wisdom upon the world. The *Dhammapada* points out that "the sun is bright by day, the moon shines by night, the warrior is bright in his armor, the meditator is bright in his meditation; but Buddha, the Awakened, is bright with splendor day and night."

These analogies to light are not applied to the historical Buddha alone but to other buddhas as well. The *Sutra on the Buddha of Eternal Life* describes the buddha Lokesvararaja as "of endless light, he lights up all regions, he the king of kings . . . O thou of immeasurable light, whose knowledge is endless and incomparable; not any other light can shine here where thou art!" When reading these descriptions, it is difficult not to be reminded of John 8:12: "I am the light of the world."

Both Buddhism and Christianity also use light as a metaphor for the true self because its nature is to illuminate. Chapter 14 of the *Record of Transmitting the Light* tells us that the solitary light (essential nature), exquisitely radiant, never darkens itself. As the wish-fulfilling pearl, as the priceless gem—it shines in various ways. The description of the heart of suchness in the *Awakening of Faith* exemplifies this.

Suchness has such characteristics as follows: the effulgence of great wisdom; the universal illumination of the universe; the true and adequate knowledge; the mind pure and clean in its self-nature.

The light that is transmitted is the Buddha wisdom, which is our birthright.

When the Buddha was asked "What is the light in the world?" he answered, "Wisdom is the light in this world." The living Jesus, too, is this wisdom shining upon all things. Like all of us, he and his disciples have come from the light, the place where light came into being on its own accord and established itself, and became manifest in image. In name Jesus and Thomas are two things, but in light they are one and the same. Without the lamp of emptiness, the lamplight of Jesus and Thomas could not shine in the *Gospel of Thomas*.

This is the same light that Zen Master Eihei Dogen spoke of when he elaborated on "the radiant light" to his disciples. For Dogen the entire world of the ten directions is our own radiant light. The self and light are equal in scope and jointly eternal. This radiant light illumines the self and the world without limits and leaves nothing hidden. This is why Jesus can rightly say in saying 30, "Lift up the stone, and you will find me there. Split a piece of wood, and I am there" because he is the light that reveals everything too.

In the chapter titled "Absorption in the Treasury of Light" of the *Treasury of the True Dharma Eye: Record of Things Heard*, Zen Master Koun Ejo wrote that the inherent nature of all things is the treasury of the great light of complete awareness. This great light of the "Lamplike Illuminate" pervades the universe and is everyone. "Even Shakyamuni and Maitreya are its servants." Jesus and his disciples are its servants, too, since the treasury of light manifested itself through their image just as it did for Shakyamuni and will do for Maitreya, the future buddha to come.

Master Ejo's words run like a Buddhist version of saying 77, which states: "I am the light shining upon all things. I am the sum of everything, for everything has come forth from me, and toward me everything unfolds." Jesus too can say "I alone am the World-Honored One." He is also the stone and the wood, and so is Thomas, and all of the disciples. The essential and the phenomenal, the one and the many harmonize perfectly.

Saying 83 reiterates this point. Images are manifest to us in our daily life. We see differentiation every second of the day. Nevertheless, there is not one moment in which the nature of anything is separate from the essential world. "The light in them remains concealed in the image of the light." The seen is always the unseen at the same time. To see what existed prior to all things is crucial to understanding the relationship between the all-pervading light and its images in saying 83.

This is not to say, of course, that just because everything is one that we are not individuals with particular characteristics. The *Lotus Sutra* explains that everything exhibits the "ten suchnesses"—they have such a form, nature, entity, ability, function, primary cause, occasion or condition, effect, recompense, and a complete fundamental whole. Despite universal oneness, everything exhibits these ten differential aspects of reality.

So our image "will become manifest" no matter which way you look at it because that is the nature of reality. At the same time, our image "will remain concealed" by or subsumed within the light of the dharmakaya as well because complete fundamental wholeness is also one of the ten key features of our world. We cannot have form without emptiness or emptiness without form.

Saying 83 can be seen as a good example of a koan that asks us to contemplate emptiness and how it operates. It could serve as what is known as a *hosshin* koan. A hosshin or dharmakaya koan functions to reveal the dharmakaya to the Zen practitioner. By sitting with these kinds of koans we can come to an understanding of the ultimate and unconditioned, what saying 50 calls "the place where light came into being by itself."

This is why finding our essential nature, the sum of everything, is likened by Buddhists to finding light. In his first discourse the Buddha announced: "Light arose in me in things not heard before." The *Flower Ornament Sutra* articulates the transformational properties of the light of the dharmakaya, the universal ground of being.

> It is even so with the dharmakaya . . . which may rightly be called the treasure of treasures, the thesaurus of all merits, and the mine of intelligence. Whoever comes in touch with this light is all transformed into the same color as that of the Buddha. Whoever sees this light, all obtain the purest eye of Dharma. Whoever comes in touch with this light rids of poverty and suffering, attains wealth and eminence, enjoys the bliss of the incomparable Bodhi.

Unsurprisingly, the *Dhammapada* recommends that a wise man should leave the dark state and follow the bright state.

Saying 50 continues this theme of actively shining like the sun. At first it concentrates on emptiness and then the phenomenal. As I pointed out before, in many koans the first question is a sassho, a checking question, often along the lines of "Where have you come from?" This is the way in which a teacher can ascertain the understanding of emptiness in the student.

In saying 50 this relationship is reversed. The disciples are asked by those lacking the wisdom eye where they have come from. These people are asking from a purely phenomenal point of view; they mean an actual place. This time it is the disciples' turn to be the teacher and to actually give the correct answer to them—"the place where the light came into being by itself [and] established itself." After this teaching on emptiness they move on to differentiation.

Saying 50 then zeroes in on the rewards of seeing the light in terms of the naturalness of actions that arise out of an understanding of the essential. The disciples are given a case scenario that asks them to consider how they will answer the question "Is the light of the father you?" They are told they must demonstrate their knowledge of the ten suchnesses and give an answer that focuses on them as individual expressions of the ultimate. So they are not to answer from the position of emptiness but differentiation.

Say that you are its child, they are told, that you are a unique configuration of the essential, the elect of the father. In other words, express the fact that you are treading the deathless path and have in that way been "chosen" (in the sense of awakening in saying 23) by the essential (the Father). If you are then asked how they can tell you are enlightened, answer that you move and rest naturally and freely, that you eat when hungry and sleep when tired.

While saying 83 might be considered a hosshin koan, saying 50 could easily be a *kikan*, or dynamic action koan. Kikan koans show that the Kingdom is not merely still and tranquil but also active and dynamic; not only is it empty and undifferentiated but it is also full of distinctions and differentiation or, as saying 50 puts it, "movement and rest." In the *Awakening of Faith* the term *Mahayana* (the "Great Vehicle" of Buddhism) is considered synonymous with suchness or the oneness of the totality of things. One of its three essential points of significance is the greatness of both the phenomenal and supra-phenomenal. This immovable essential is what moves us to act. All movement is within stillness and vice versa. In Zen this is known as the great activity. It is the active aspect of the essential that "produces all kinds of good work in the world." It is said that when we have awareness of oneness with all, and take each thing as complete in itself, the great activity appears.

Zen Master Linji Yixuan spoke of the "true man of no rank," a term for the true self, the person who is present in every particle of our life's activity. This person is at the base or source of this activity, so that action, wisdom, seeing, resting, and knowing are as one. This refers to the movement of emptiness, since where there is not a single thing there is great activity. Since great action is totally unbound by convention, it is also said that "the wheel of activity has no obstruction." It is an appropriate response to the here and now without the obstruction of ego or convention.

As for rest and repose, in saying 2 Jesus recommends one kind of "rest," that is, illumination of the true nature of reality, the manifestation of perfect rest. Saying 50 couples movement and rest together and in doing so shows us another kind of rest—the counterbalance to action in the world. We know when to act and when not to. This is the insightful naturalness of the plowman in saying 109 who found his treasure and used it.

Known in Japanese Zen Buddhism as *kufu*, this kind of rest or ease is the naturalness in bodily action that comes about when we perform an action without our own ego or self-predilections standing in the way. A realized disciple feels that acting naturally and in accordance with their essential nature is true wisdom. When we do this we are free to respond and free to rest.

This is how Jesus can truthfully say in saying 90 "my yoke is easy and my requirements are light. You'll be refreshed." This lifting of the burden of the human condition is found in Buddhism by going into the yoke with Buddha, by believing in and enacting the Dharma. This yoke is not really a yoke but true lightness of being. This is not the eternal rest attained after death but repose in the present, a fact that *Thomas*, true to its theme and purpose, constantly repeats.

Sayings 50, 77, 83, and 90 echo the words of Zen Master Jianfu Chenggu: When you look into a saying continuously, you discover the light and everything is completely revealed. This is how to treat all the sayings of the *Gospel of Thomas*. They reveal their wisdom light when we discover our own. The Buddha's last words encouraged us to become a lamp to others, but they might very well have been, "To become a realized person, a bringer of light, why do you not seek a light?" Sayings 50, 77, 83, and 90 say no different.

29

LET YOUR LIGHT SHINE

His disciples said, "Show us the place where you are, because we need to look for it." He said to them, "Anyone who has ears to hear should hear! Light exists within a person of light, and they light up the whole world. If they don't shine, there's darkness."

—*Gospel of Thomas*, saying 24

We must carry an iron yoke with no hole, it is not a slight matter, the curse is passed on to our descendants. If you want to support the gate and sustain the house, you must climb a mountain of swords with bare feet.

—*Gateless Gate*, case 17

Sayings 24 looks at the ramifications of gaining insight into the true self. It suggests that, as an expression of community fellowship, we must all help each other along the Way. Moreover, upon discovering the Kingdom, we must not withhold our knowledge from others or seek to stifle our essential self by failing to act upon it when the situation requires. Such a failure suppresses the spiritual development of both ourselves and others, as well as failing to implement skillful means in a judicious manner.

In saying 24, the disciples are at it again. In koan literature it is the head monk who serves as the foil to the wise teacher. We would expect such a person as the head monk to demonstrate great insight, but the reverse is usually the case in most koans. So it is with the disciples. They would fit well into Zen literature.

This time they ask Jesus to show them the actual place where he is because they need to find it for true movement and repose to occur (sayings 50 and 90). The plus side of this is that they know enough to realize that they don't know some sort of key information. At the same time, they have still not realized that the Kingdom is here and now.

Jesus asks them to listen up. He skillfully avoids giving specific details but says, "Light exists within a person of light, and they light up the whole world. If they don't shine, there's darkness." What is Jesus doing here? First, we could see this as Jesus hinting that the "place" of enlightenment is both within and without. Second, he is directing their attention to their own essential nature that lights up the whole universe. Third, he is suggesting that when we either don't see this or we deny it, then that is a loss to everyone. And last, he suggests that the continuance of a spiritual tradition is dependent upon people spreading its good news.

If we take the last one for example, sayings 24 and 33 make clear that Jesus wants the secrets of the deathless not to be lost in the annals of history. He would like this not only for the sake of continuance but out of compassion for humanity as well. In the Digha Nikaya the Buddha, too, had this concern.

> Monks, you should carefully assume those practices which I have taught for the sake of direct knowledge. You should practice them, cultivate them, and make much of them, so that this religious practice will last for a long time.

Like Jesus, the Buddha also sent his disciples out to spread the good news. His instructions contain an energy and intent similar to sayings 24 and 35. In the Vinaya, the regulatory framework for the monastic community, it is said that he told this to the monks: "You should shine forth."

In Zen the responsibility for continuance of the lineage has traditionally been very important. Both case 17, "Chu the National Teacher Gives Three Calls," and case 6, "Guishan Lingyou Kicks Over the Water Pitcher," of the *Gateless Gate* emphasize the seriousness of this task. In case 17 Wumen Huikai makes the following observation: "We must carry an iron yoke with no hole, it is not a slight matter, the curse is passed on to our descendants; If you want to support the gate and sustain the house, you must climb a mountain of swords with bare feet." In saying 90 Jesus says, "Come to me because my yoke is easy." Zen would have no problem with this kind of yoke since it expresses the lightness of being that a complete sense of the Kingdom brings. It is the iron yoke with no hole that is hard to use.

Wumen was commenting on the responsibility of passing on the Zen lineage given to Chu (Huizhong), the national teacher. This responsibility is a yoke, but it is no ordinary one—it is made of iron and has no hole for the head to go through. Case 17 is a good example of Zen irony since it is a way of saying that to pass on the teachings is a serious and heavy responsibility, almost an impossible task or a curse because of the weight of its importance. Yet it is also a joyous and liberating one. So if we want to pass the teachings on to our descendants in the Dharma, we must take this responsibility seriously and continue our mission despite the difficulties, even if we have to "climb a mountain of swords with bare feet." It is similar to taking up Jesus's cross of understanding in saying 55.

Case 6 suggests that we take the towel band from our head and put on an iron yoke. In saying this, Wumen was commenting on the decision by Zen Master Guishan Lingyou to teach. He refers to the action of putting aside reticence and reservations (the towel band) and getting down to the actual nitty gritty.

In case 61, "Fengxue's One Atom of Dust" of the *Blue Cliff Record*, Fengxue Yanzhao instructed, "If a single grain of dust is raised, the nation prospers. If a single grain of dust is not raised, the nation perishes." Xuetou Chongxian held out his staff and said, "Are there after all any monks who live together and die together with this?"

There are three possible interpretations of this case. First, if we cling to concepts (the speck of dust), separate things exist. If we do not, there is only the great void. Second, when we awaken (raise the speck of dust), we see the whole phenomenal world in the fullness of emptiness. If we don't, then we don't see the world as it is. Lastly, and this is most relevant to saying 24, for the teaching to prosper, doctrines, schools, and traditions are developed (the dust raised). While these are very useful, if we cling to these things or think they are anything but the finger pointing to the moon, and not the moon itself, the teaching dies. We ourselves must be the teaching; this is the best method by which it continues.

A mind of division, however, is not conducive to the development of true loving-kindness. The *25,000-Line Perfection of Wisdom Sutra* alludes to the proper state of mind an awakened person must have. It makes a comparison between the Buddha's disciples and glowworms. A glowworm, being a mere insect, does not think that its light could illuminate the world or shine over it. Yet it shines in the darkness. So too does the sun, when it has risen, shed its light over everything. So just by virtue of being themselves (like people who know their true self), they bring about understanding in others.

The full expression of our true self lights up the whole universe as a matter of course (saying 24). Through both the natural and free-flowing expression of realization, and specific and targeted activities, such people help others to lessen their suffering and ignorance. The *Awakening of Faith* expresses this idea of connectivity through the light of wisdom. It states that when a Buddha Land is founded upon the pure mind of a single person, that single pure mind draws other similar minds to itself. In this way, faith in the Buddha spreads from individual to family, from family to village, and finally to the whole world. As the light of a small candle will spread from one to another in succession, so the light of Buddha's compassion will pass on from one mind to another endlessly.

The disciples yet again do not seem to have imbibed this knowledge. Perhaps they were thinking of future events in which the light of the Kingdom would come down from upon high. To ask where Jesus is betrays a limited understanding not only of the light within them, but also the illuminating and all-pervading function of that light.

Not one to give up, in saying 33 Jesus asks the disciples to proclaim from their rooftops that the door to the deathless is open: "What you will hear in your ear, in the other ear proclaim from your rooftops. After all, no one lights a lamp and puts it under a basket, nor does one put it in a hidden place. Rather, one puts it on a lampstand so that all who come and go will see its light." He is saying that when you have the lamp of wisdom don't hide it. As the expression of our true self, put it on display so that all may benefit.

This notion is expressed in the Udana, which points out that an awakened person is like "a man who, having eyes and bearing a lamp, sees all objects, is he who has heard the law of vice and virtue; he will become perfectly wise." His wisdom is his natural way of preaching from the rooftops. Jesus is trying to elicit contemplation of the timeless and borderless nature of the Kingdom, which is that no one is actually "outside" the system and left in the dark.

This is why traditionally in Mahayana Buddhism not to assist others in religious maturation flies in the face of the fact that it is only together with others that we fully learn to fathom the reality of all existence. In "Skillful Means," chapter 2 of the *Lotus Sutra*, the Buddha explained that the wisdom of buddhas is extremely deep and infinite and difficult to enter and understand. For this reason, "only a buddha together with a buddha" can fathom the reality of all existence.

To learn from good companions and good teachings on the Way is not just half of the Way, the Buddha said; it is the whole of it. Some things are just bigger than us alone, and we need help to fully understand them.

Since everything in the Kingdom is connected, everything is defined by its relationship. Realizing true nature together with another living one reflects the interrelational aspect of the Kingdom.

To also withhold the skillful expression of one's nature on purpose is in essence not properly utilizing the interconnected nature of reality. The Anguttara Nikaya urges us to strive with effort if we see that something is for our own benefit, another's benefit, or benefit for both. What this is pointing out is that, as a mirror of deeper principles, understanding requires relationship. This is as much for ourselves as others.

It may be that everything is the Kingdom, but it still remains that the assistance and inspiration of other people is needed for a mature understanding to develop. This is why it is commonly believed in the Zen school that a student and teacher awaken together. Awakening is both a solitary and communal act. We awaken in this body but also as the cosmic body. Emptiness entails that everything awakens when we do (because everything is interconnected) but that our individual practice is also deepened and refined through interaction with other people.

Since "wisdom is difficult to enter and to understand," we need others along the way to help clarify and encourage our journey. Anyone who thinks that they do not need any input from others is not doing themselves any favors and placing extra pressure on themselves. Likewise, withholding assistance (in any form) for nonvirtuous reasons runs contrary to this principle as well.

As I said in the prologue, the sayings of this gospel are secret in the sense that they are obscure and difficult to understand. This doesn't mean that they are to be kept secret. Saying 33 clearly states that the *Gospel of Thomas* is to be made known to all. This is not to say, however, that it is unreasonable to assume that all sorts of things can rightly and reasonably prevent a person from doing this. What it is suggesting is that we should make the most of opportunities as they present themselves and whenever we feel confident in doing so. This is what saying 24 is intimating, too.

Saying 33 also adds another element to the equation. "What you will hear in your ear, in the other ear proclaim from your rooftops." What this is saying is that we must first awaken our "inner ear" and then try our utmost to reflect what we know through our own physical eyes and ears. Both inner and outer "hearing" have a place in the Kingdom. A beacon of light shines its light outward, but it must be activated first to be of any use.

Listening with the ear of wisdom is traditionally regarded in Buddhism as "listening beyond the ear." This is the effort to attain the correct understanding of the nature of the self through deep listening and skillful consideration. In Zen it is the recognition of emptiness as "sound and listening" itself. It is this which causes the Dharma ear to arise within people. The classic and oft-repeated koan "What is the sound of one hand" is designed to do precisely this. Knowing the answer to this koan entails knowing that in oneness any sound, indeed any sight, taste, touch, and feeling, is that very same sound.

So acting from essential nature is the necessary condition for the propagation of a teaching since without it, engagement only increases the power of the separate self. Zen Master Linji Yixuan spoke of the boundless nature of the light within a man of light, and why he lights up the whole world. He strongly reminded his students that it was urgently important for them to realize the one who manipulates light. What is it that can speak and listen to the Dharma? he asked his disciples. It's none other than *this*, a solitary brightness standing right in front of us.

It is *this* (that is, emptiness) we must trust. In the Zen text titled the *Breakthrough Sermon*, Bodhidharma, who is believed to have transmitted Zen from India to China, drew an analogy between an aware and enlightened person and an eternal lamp lighting up the darkness. By passing the Dharma on to others, enlightened people are able to use one lamp to light thousands of lamps. Since these lamps then light countless other lamps, their light lasts forever.

This is why some translations of saying 24 do not say "If it does not shine it is dark" but "If they don't shine, there's darkness." If a person does not show and express his attainment, then what is its practical use? As the old adage suggests, we must use it or lose it. It is possible to lose complete touch with our own nature, and that would be a dark day indeed. The man of light can become a man of darkness, which suggests that his illumination of the world is not automatic. It takes effort and vigilance.

Sayings 24, 33, and 35 urge us to discover our own light in order to discover everyone else's. It is said in Zen that when we reach the stage of realizing there is essentially no one to save, that it is all the light of the Kingdom, but we must not remain in that realization. Instead, we must build upon that insight and continue unfolding our true nature. Moreover, we should be skillful in how we do this, making use of opportune moments and adept methods as best we can. As John 12:35 suggests, "Walk while you have the light, that darkness may not overtake you . . . he who walks in the darkness does not know where he goes."

30

STINGINESS

Jesus said, "The Pharisees and the scholars have taken the keys of knowledge and hidden them. They haven't entered, and haven't let others enter who wanted to. So be wise as serpents and innocent as doves."

—*Gospel of Thomas*, saying 39

When Master Yunyan Tansheng asked Daowu Yuanzhi, "How does the Bodhisattva use all those many hands and eyes?" Yuanzhi said, "It is like a person groping for his pillow in the middle of the night."

—*Blue Cliff Record*, case 89

Saying 39 tells us that we should endeavor not to be stingy and withholding. In fact, this saying is highly ironic. The Pharisees and scholars are usually believed to be ignorant of the truth. They corrupt the teachings and abuse their power. In this saying, however, it is assumed that they have the keys of knowledge but have hidden them. The proper question to ask here is not how is this so but how can it not be so? Like everyone, they are the Kingdom, so of course they have the keys to knowledge. It is an innate principle within every fiber of our being.

The main problem is their ignorance and willful denial of it. They are selfish and restrict knowledge of the true self both to themselves and to other people. This is the ultimate failure as a teacher. Not only do they refuse to "shine on the whole world," but they can't even administer properly to themselves. They have not suitably utilized their possession of the keys, and they will let no one else use them either. The ego-self reigns supreme.

One of the Zen bodhisattva precepts mentioned in chapter 26 is the precept of not being stingy or encouraging others to be so. The *Brahma Net Sutra* explains that a disciple of the Buddha must not act in a stingy manner, encourage others to do so, or involve themselves in the causes, conditions, methods, or karma of stinginess. When encountering a poor or destitute person, for example, a bodhisattva should not refuse to give them "even a coin, a needle, or a blade of grass, or to speak even a sentence, a verse or a dust's worth of dharma." If they have hateful or nasty thoughts about that person and then scold and humiliate them, they commit a major offense.

This guideline is expressed in various ways such as "There is no miserliness," "Do not be covetous," or more commonly, "Not sparing the Dharma assets." The Dharma assets are the actual teachings, but they are also "the ten thousand things and one hundred grasses" or the "one Dharma." In other words, the entire Kingdom. It has never lacked anything, so stinginess is not actually in its nature. Since the Kingdom is the eternal all-pervading light, we must realize how inexhaustible it is in order to enact and eventually become the precept.

To not use everything at our disposal is to foster the mind of poverty in ourselves and others. This is another aspect of this precept—if we are stingy with our gifts and actions, this not only affects ourselves, it models and creates a stingy atmosphere in general. Again, helping yourself is to help others. This is a fact the Pharisees and the scholars seem to have forgotten.

The precept against miserliness is reiterated in saying 105 when Jesus says, "How awful for the Pharisees who are like a dog sleeping in a feeding trough for cattle, because the dog doesn't eat, and [doesn't let] the cattle eat either." The Pharisees are compared to animals with a single-minded and selfish purpose who refuse themselves and others sustenance. They begrudge the natural appetite for enlightenment that exists within us. No wonder Jesus cites them as an example of what not to do.

He suggests that we be as shrewd as snakes and innocent as doves instead. This seems to suggest that an awakened person who wants to enlighten others must not take an absolute stance like the Pharisees and scholars. To display the light openly (saying 32 and 33) there are times when it is prudent to speak of the essential "unseen" (saying 5) and times when it is more appropriate to speak from a purely phenomenal viewpoint—the snake and the dove coexist. We do that when we react with the appropriateness that comes with wisdom. Sometimes it is better to speak of matters that are deep and not easily understood, and sometimes we must just let the words issue forth from essential nature.

When the Buddha attained enlightenment underneath the bodhi tree, he deliberated over whether to tell others about it. At first he decided it was more skillful to keep silent and to refrain from trying to communicate his insight to others. He initially thought that his audience wouldn't understand, since realization cannot be fully described in words. He felt that they would turn a deaf ear to his message. After a time however, he changed his mind.

His solution was upaya. Known in Buddhism as skillful or expedient means, upaya is the appropriate response or interaction to the situation at hand. Case 89, "The Hands and Eyes of the Bodhisattva of Great Compassion" of the *Blue Cliff Record*, demonstrates upaya aptly. In this koan Avalokiteshvara, a humanlike archetype of compassion, appears with his symbolic multitude of hands ready to help all and sundry. When Master Yunyan Tansheng asked Daowu Yuanzhi, "How does the

Bodhisattva use all those many hands and eyes?" Yuanzhi said, "It is like a person groping for his pillow in the middle of the night."

This is the perfect expression of an awakened heart-mind—reaching back automatically to adjust the pillow. That's the nature of upaya and of awakening. The more a person becomes free from the reign of the self, the more natural upaya becomes, and the more Avalokiteshvara's arms become our own. Put simply, it is the flexible and harmless use of anything that demonstrates the truth of emptiness. The implication here is that even if a technique or view is unorthodox it can still be expedient if it brings a person closer to the realization. Upaya is the use of the best possible provisional strategies in any given situation to express the Dharma. In Zen *mondos* (recorded dialogues between a student and a teacher) and koans are an example of this.

In case 14, "Yunmen's Appropriate Statement" of the *Blue Cliff Record*, a monk asked Zen Master Yunmen Wenyan, "What are the 'periods and teachings' of the whole lifetime of Shakyamuni?" Yunmen said, "A preaching in accordance" (that is, an appropriate statement). The monk was asking about the essence of the Buddha's teaching during his lifetime. Master Yunmen answered that it can be summed up by one thing—upaya—the skillful and appropriate application of the Dharma. As I mentioned previously, the Buddha was so skilled in upaya that he could quickly adapt his style and content to suit his audience. He spoke to and aroused the mind of enlightenment in a wide variety of people.

Unsurprisingly, in Zen upaya is a virtue in itself. It is both the method of getting the message across to people and, as one of the ten perfections or *paramitas*, the natural expression of a virtuous person's life. These perfections refer to the perfection or culmination of ten key virtues that characterize an enlightened state: generosity, morality, patience, energy, concentration, skillful means, aspiration, spiritual power, knowledge, and wisdom. The perfection of wisdom and the use of skillful means are considered to be mutually dependent since an enlightened person's perfections do not allow them to act in any way other than skillfully.

Jesus fully demonstrated this fact. He always carefully chose when, where, and how to speak. Sometimes he was also silent purely because his audience would not have understood what he said. In 1 Corinthians 3:1 Jesus pointed out that the spiritually undeveloped man cannot receive the things of the Spirit and neither can he know them, because they are spiritually discerned. In Buddhism appropriately withholding speech is called "noble silence."

He kept in mind the basic principle outlined in Proverbs 15:23: "A person finds joy in giving an apt reply—and how good is a timely word!" For this reason, in the *Gospel of Thomas* he drew upon the analogy of a snake and a dove to symbolize the necessity of a balanced and utilitarian approach to spiritual matters. Sometimes we must be forceful and direct, at other times gentle and unassuming, and sometimes we must be completely silent.

Sayings 39 and 105 can be used to remind ourselves that we should try our best not to feel some sort of negativity toward those who have a limited understanding of the Kingdom. Theragatha 1,026 reminds us that an awakened person who despises someone who is not is "like a blind man walking around with a torch in his hand." This is a traditional Buddhist way of saying "be the change you wish to see in the world." It is pointing out that when we have the means to improve someone's lot in life then it can be a shame not to use it. Rather than complaining, we should act.

31

BODIES

Jesus said, "Whoever has known the system has mastered the body—and whoever has found the body, of him the system is not worthy."

—*Gospel of Thomas*, saying 80

One day, Daowu Yuanzhi appeared in the lecture hall with a hoe and walked from east to west and from west to east. Shishuang Qingzhu said, "What are you doing?" Daowu Yuanzhi said, "I am seeking the sacred bones of our late master." Shishuang Qingzhu said, "On the billows of the great ocean, whitecaps swell to the sky. What sacred bones of our late master are you looking for?" Daowu Yuanzhi said, "That is good for my training." Deshan Xuanjian said, "The sacred bones of our late master still exist."

—*Blue Cliff Record*, case 55

Saying 80 addresses the role of the body in religious practice. It suggests that instead of rejecting the body, we can put it in its proper perspective. This involves positioning it correctly in relation to the essential nature of the Kingdom. It is not separate, lower, or somehow dirtier than the eternal. When we realize that the body (or the phenomenal world in general) is one part of the Kingdom—and not the only part—then we have what it takes to become a living one.

So what is saying 80 actually saying about our bodies? It announces that "whoever has known the system has mastered the body—and whoever has found the body, of him the system is not worthy." The word *system* has also been translated as "world" (meaning the conventional, material world), and *light* has often been used instead of *body*. So an alternative reading might be "he who has known the world has found the light, but he who has found the light, the world is not worthy of him."

The first half of this saying is the focus of saying 7—mastering the kleshas. As I've explained in chapter 11, this is one strategy for creating the conditions that promote realization. So whoever has mastered the body and the phenomenal world is in a good position to enter the Kingdom. In the second half of saying 7, the "body" Jesus is talking about is the Kingdom, the cosmic body of Christ, he who fills the universe in all its parts. Saying 24 tells us that this is the light of wisdom that permeates the Kingdom. So in knowing the light we know that our bodies are the cosmic body.

In Digha Nikaya 16, the Buddha took a lot of time to explain that death is only the physical end of the body. The true body is enlightenment. A human body must die but the wisdom of enlightenment will exist forever. Zen Master Hakuin Ekaku, who devised rigorous training methods integrating meditation and koan practice, pointed out in the *Song of Zazen* that this very place is the lotus land, this very body, the Buddha. This knowledge means that the world is not worthy of us, an ironic statement meaning that a way of life built upon just material and intellectual structures cannot hope to match this insight of a living one. It simply can't equal the light of the Kingdom.

Case 55 of the *Blue Cliff Record* deals with this expanded sense of body. It starts with a monk who is marching up and down in the meditation hall with a hoe in his hand and staring intently from side to side. He is trying to demonstrate the fact that essential nature includes everything, even such actions as walking with a hoe in a hall. Unfortunately, this is a bit grandiose, which is confirmed when he says that he is looking for the remains of his departed master.

Shishuang Qingzhu says to him, "On the billows of the great ocean, whitecaps swell to the sky. What sacred bones of our late master are you looking for?" This is giving him a hint that nothing is separate from us, even the bones of the late master, which in this case is a metaphor for essential nature. Qingzhu is trying to create the imagery of waves rising and falling, just as in our daily lives we stand up, sit down, sleep and rise, eat and drink. If the Dharma body can't be found there, then where else can it be? It is everything here and now.

All of these things are the bones of the late master, just as everything is the Kingdom. Our essential nature is not different or separate from the nature of the phenomenal world. Recognizing the wisdom in this, Daowu Yuanzhi comments that that was good for his practice. Deshan Xuanjian observes that if Yuanzhi finally gets it, "The sacred bones of our late master still exist."

Recognizing the body as suchness also lends itself to the realization that the cosmic body is a purified analogue of our own body. This puts our body into its proper and wider place as we realize that it is far more than just a particular and individual configuration and more than just physical. We are the cosmic body of the Kingdom. So there are also bodily realities that are nonphysical. The "body" is more than just the gross physical form.

Case 9 of the *Gateless Gate* states that far better than realizing the body is to realize the heart-mind and be at peace. If the heart-mind is realized, there is no anxiety about the body. If both body and heart-mind are completely realized, a holy hermit does not wish to be appointed lord. In this case the heart-mind refers to the totality of what is experienced by the heart and mind together. In other words, suchness.

It is saying that if we see the essential then the phenomenal falls into place, but if we just see the phenomenal we get caught in concepts and materiality and can't see the true nature of reality. The last two lines refer to the fact that when we put the body and the cosmic body in their proper places then we do not think ourselves special. We're happy to be an ordinary person.

The benefit of this attitude is that we can come to see that life is the unity of the physical and the spiritual. There is no way that embodiment prevents anyone from uniting with the ultimate, because the truth of emptiness means no separation between anything. The physical and spiritual are seamlessly joined, and because of this we don't have to seek solutions to our pain through damaging strategies such as suppressing sexuality and the body or dividing matter and spirit.

Saying 80 is the exact opposite of *contemptus mundi*, a medieval theology that stressed the corruptibility of the soul by the sinful human will. Although the notion of contemptus mundi was designed to prevent undue attachment to physicality, it was more often than not enacted as a severe rejection of the body and its sensuality. But if we position the phenomenal within and together with the essential, then in the Kingdom we simply can't siphon off the body and be left with the eternal. They are one and the same.

The implication of this unity is that since the world of experience is within our own bodies, if we understand the body in both its material and ultimate senses, then we understand the world, for everything is interconnected and empty. As the Buddha once said, "In this very fathom-long body, endowed with perception and mind, I declare the world, the arising of the world, the ending of the world, and the way leading to the ending of the world."

32

THE ASTRINGENT PERSIMMON

Jesus said, "There was a rich man who had much money. He said, 'I'll use my money to sow, reap, plant, and fill my barns with fruit, so that I won't need anything.' That's what he was thinking to himself, but he died that very night. Anyone who has ears to hear should hear!"

—*Gospel of Thomas*, saying 63

"These children are mine, these riches are mine"; with these thoughts is the fool disturbed. What are children and riches to one who owns not even himself in the other world? It is the law of humanity that, though one acquires hundreds and thousands of worldly goods, one still falls into the power of the lord of death.

—Udanavarga 1.20–21

This saying deals with poverty and wealth, and the appropriate view of them held by a wise person. It looks at these two issues in mainly a material sense and not a spiritual one. *Thomas*, as usual, puts its own spin on this.

In saying 63 we have a clear example of a lesson about the use of money. In it we have a rich man who stores up all his possessions for a rainy day but dies before that day comes. His intention is to lack nothing, but in the end he is deprived of his own life. It is this intention that is the key to understanding this saying. Rather than an outright injunction against material wealth, this saying concerns priorities and the proper use of acquisitions.

In terms of priorities we can see that the storehouse of produce is not the storehouse this man should be concentrating on—the storehouse of the heart-mind mentioned in saying 45. If this were the case, the man would be able to see that wealth is not necessarily a problem in itself but it can be in the way that it is used. If the intention with which it is acquired is not within an ethical and realized framework, then it leads to bad karma, and ironically the amassed wealth can outlast the person who acquires it.

Like Thomas, the Buddha did not denounce wealth and material gain outright. There were times when he taught that there were dangers in wealth and to cast it aside, but he also pointed out that there are circumstances in which it promotes well-being. If there is one overarching theme he taught, it was that wealth in itself is not a problem, but attachment to it is. Wealth gained in ways that are unethical and conducive to bad karma is also a problem.

It is possible, he pointed out, to enjoy pleasurable things if we abandon the craving for them. In the *Aputtaka Sutta 1* the Buddha clearly stated that wealth can be enjoyed. As in saying 63, he does not moralistically denounce anyone who is misusing wealth but argues for its proper appreciation and usefulness. In this sutra the Buddha's warnings regard a rich person who dies heirless and intestate, his wealth forfeit to the crown. Like saying 63, this is used as an example of the fact that wealth has a practical value, but is useless if simply stored away.

The foolish person, in this sutra called the "false individual," does not enjoy his wealth at all, and loses everything in the end. The wise or "true individual" not only enjoys his wealth and benefits others, but safeguards it from being seized by the authorities or thieves, from being destroyed by the elements, and from being wasted away by incompetent heirs.

Grasping, craving, and acquiring in order to fill our rooms with things useful only for a day that never comes are an exercise in futility, because it is always the eternal now. The *Dhammapada* gives a clear description of the futility of acquisitiveness:

"Here I shall dwell in the rain, here in winter and summer," thus the fool meditates, and does not think of his death. Death comes and carries off that man, praised for his children and flocks, his mind distracted, as a flood carries off a sleeping village. Sons are no help, nor a father, nor relations; there is no help from kinsfolk for one whom death has seized. A wise and good man who knows the meaning of this, should quickly clear the way that leads to Nirvana.

Thanissaro Bhikkhu has the most wonderful turn of phrase in his translation of the line about the person praised for his children and flocks: "That drunk-on-his-sons-and-cattle man." The imagery is striking. We can imagine a wealthy tycoon on the front porch of his country mansion congratulating himself on his empire, not knowing that everything is empty and impermanent.

Saying 63 is also a story about hoarding our possessions and wealth and the drawbacks of stinginess. The man hoards for himself, not for the benefit of others. He has either willfully ignored or is ignorant of the fact that prosperity should never be an end in itself, but a means to some wholesome purpose. Consequently, the Buddha advised that riches that are not rightly utilized run to waste, not to enjoyment.

In chapter 30 I mentioned the Zen precept of "Not sparing the Dharma assets." If we foster the mind of acquisition in ourselves and others, it reinforces the bond of the separate self. The Dharma assets are restricted. So not only should we seek wealth lawfully and honestly, making use of it while mindful of its dangers, but we should also try our best to share it with others. If we put our wealth to good use for ourselves and others, the Buddha taught, we are happy in both this world and the next.

The Udanavarga asks us how we can have a sense of ownership of children and riches when we don't even "own" ourselves. Like the man in saying 63, those ignorant of the proper use of wealth are also ignorant of the fact that on an ultimate level, ownership is a fallacy. We do not own even ourselves in this or any other world. This is the recognition of emptiness—that there is no one to enjoy things and no things to enjoy. True wealth is a state of being.

What the Buddha is talking about is the renunciation of self because where there is a self there is what belongs to a self and vice versa. To jar us out of this delusion of separation between subject and object, in Majjhima Nikaya 22 the Buddha suggested that we must foster the wisdom that knows that "this is not mine, this am I not, this is not my self."

In chapter 21 I mentioned the "lone dweller," the one who knows that realization and renunciation are the same. Renouncing the self is the hardest of things to do, but when one has, then we know that in emptiness we lack nothing. For this reason, in *Zen Monastic Regulations*, Changlu Zongze states that "all the buddhas of the past, present, and future have renounced the world and found their true Way."

This does not involve cutting off the world, but cutting off delusion itself. While saying 63 is about the mistaken idea that material investment prevents suffering, it is also about greed—for certainty, for abundance, and for protection from the world. The Buddha's own backstory provides an example of where this can go wrong. His father, a rich man, sought to protect young Gotama from the vicissitudes of life and so showered him with every extravagance.

When he ventured out of his palace one day, he was confronted with the realities of life in the form of an aged person, a sick person, a corpse, and an ascetic. This led to the realization that the world contains deep suffering that no indulgence could prevent. This is how the rags-to-riches story was inverted by the Buddha—he left his storehouse of luxury for the wealth of enlightenment.

As for greed, it is one of the poisons or kleshas mentioned in chapter 23. The three poisons in Buddhism refer to greed, anger, and ignorance. They are called poisons because they poison our lives and prevent realization. In the *Jatakamala* the Buddha observed that, as a rule, riches joined with covetousness can be called caravans on the road toward wretchedness. This is due to the fact that greed is misplaced desire. In order to feel fulfilled, whole, and complete we mistakenly think that the objects of our desire can give this to us, not just for a while, but forever.

We grasp for happiness and satisfaction outside of ourselves. Like the man in saying 63, we think that if we just build up enough things then everything will be all right. This, of course, completely ignores the fact that there will always be a measure of suffering in the world. As long as there is the dualism of "mine" and "theirs," delusion about the nature of reality will prevail, and we will always be striving toward an unattainable goal. The solution is to see through the illusion.

In the *Wake-Up Sermon*, Bodhidharma examines the factors necessary for realization. He states that by leaving greed, anger, and delusion we can move to the realms of morality, meditation, and wisdom. Not creating delusion is enlightenment. When thoughts of greed, anger, and delusion occur, we actually become them. By *thoughts* he means conceptualization (wrong view) and so is speaking of entering the mind of nonduality that sees no separation between self and others (right view).

By returning to our original state we can disempower the three poisons. This is the "one true samadhi that extinguishes evils" mentioned by Zen Master Hakuin Ekaku. In his *Samadhi of the Self* Zen Master Menzan Zuiho makes a very useful analogy. The three poisons are like an astringent persimmon, while the threefold precepts (not to create evil, to practice good, and to actualize good for others) taught by the Buddha are like a sweet, dried persimmon. So if we leave the astringent persimmon, it rots, but if we peel and dry it carefully, it becomes a dried persimmon with a sweet taste.

Similarly, if we just let the three poisons simply be as they are, they only grow worse. If we cut the bitter persimmon up and eat it, we get a bitter taste in our mouth. If however we recognize that the astringent persimmon and the sweet persimmon are one persimmon, then the sweet taste does not appear by taking away the astringent taste. Rather, it is transformed through exposure to the light of wisdom. Again, like the lion and the man in saying 7, this is about integration and synthesis.

The rich person of saying 63 did not learn this lesson. He did not transform his greed into a state of no-suffering but instead fed it with more and more things. In accumulating his wealth and not using it appropriately he also accumulated the three poisons. He was concerned about not lacking anything material, but what he needed to do was be poor in his desires. Unfortunately, this was what he was thinking in his heart. And in that night he died. Whoever has ears should hear.

33

TRUE RICHES AND POVERTY

Why did you come out into the wilderness? To see a reed
blown about by the wind? A man dressed in soft raiment like
your rulers and the powerful? Yes, indeed, they are clothed
in fine, luxurious garments, but what they lack is the ability
to discern truth.

—*Gospel of Thomas*, saying 78

After Shishuang Qingzhu's passing, the assembly wanted to
appoint their head monk as the abbot of the temple. Jiufeng
would not acknowledge him. He said, "Wait till I examine
him. If he understands our late master's spirit and intention,
I will serve him as I served our late master." So he gave the
head monk some words of the late teacher and said, "Tell me,
what sort of matter did he clarify with this?"

The head monk said, "He clarified the matter of the One
Color." Jiufeng said, "If so, you have not yet understood our
late master's spirit." The head monk said, "Don't you acknowledge me? Pass me incense." He lit the incense and said, "If
I had not understood our late master's spirit, I would not
be able to pass away while the smoke of this incense rises."
No sooner had he said this than he expired while sitting in
meditation. Jiufeng caressed his back and said, "Dying while

sitting or standing is not impossible. But you could not even dream of our late master's spirit."

—*Book of Equanimity*, case 96

S aying 78 relates to metaphorical and spiritual matters rather than material ones. The wealth of the Kingdom is its essential nature so that both the riches of wisdom and the poverty of nonconceptualization bring great benefit to a person in the here and now.

It is obvious in saying 78 that the people Jesus is addressing have not shed light upon their own preconceptions about him and the Kingdom. What did you expect to see, he asks them. Fireworks? A big show of things? Some freaky mysterious thing like a reed suddenly shaken by the wind? Trendy clothes like really rich people wear? Well, he says, they have mighty fine garments, but they are still unable to discern the truth. Their clothes haven't got them on the red carpet of the Kingdom. After all, as the *Dhammapada* reminds us, what good are fine garments and great hair when within yourself everything is messy? Why polish the exterior when the interior needs work?

One of my favorite Zen stories about Ikkyu Sojun, an eccentric Zen monk and poet, concerns fine garments. One day, wealthy patrons invited Ikkyu to a banquet. He arrived dressed in his beggar's robes. The host, thinking he was some itinerant bum, shooed him off. So Ikkyu went home and changed into his fine priestly regalia. When he arrived there was much fanfare, and he was received into the banquet room. Once inside he put his robe on the cushion and left, saying, "Well, I expect you invited the robe since you showed me away a little while ago." I wish I had been there to see their faces. They obviously did not see what the Buddha saw in Udanavarga 30.17–18: that "those whose minds delight in contemplation, they wear the garment of the law."

The Buddha himself, having grown up a prince of sorts, admitted his own penchant for fine things in his youth. In the Anguttara Nikaya he said, "I was very delicately nurtured."

> In my father's home there was a pond for blue lotuses, another for red lotuses and one other for white lotuses and all of them for my sake. I never used sandals other than from Benares. My head dress, close fitting jacket, garment and the outer robe were all from Benares cloth. A white parasol was held over me day and night, with the intention, may cold, heat, dust, grass or dew drops not touch him. There were three mansions for me, one for winter, one for summer and the other for the rains.

He obviously lived in total refinement until that fateful day he realized that this had not made him happy at all. No wonder he had a dim view of miracles and showmanship, the reed shaken by the wind.

In fact, at one time, the Majjhima Nikaya tells us, a monk called Sunakkhatta left the monkhood purely because "the recluse Gotama does not have any superhuman states" and because the Buddha would not perform miracles for him. The Buddha did not deny the reality of such experiences, but he pointed out that the only reliable miracle is the miracle of instruction in the Dharma. The rest is just for show.

The people in saying 78 are clothed in conceptualizations. They want to see a big show. They have come all the way out to the wilderness perhaps in search of something "purer" than their city-living lifestyle. Maybe they think this "back to the country" move will bring a simpler, and therefore, "better" answer to the ills of life. What a lot of baggage to carry around!

Unfortunately, Zen is still sometimes afflicted with this obsession with flashy superpowers. The myth of the Zen master as someone who sees all and knows all had led to a variety of elevated expectations about what Zen practice actually is. This was no different in earlier times. In several koans and stories students question teachers about the powers they think they will attain through Zen.

In case 96 of the *Book of Equanimity* the story is told of Jiufeng, who served Shishuang Qingzhu as his attendant:

> After Shishuang Qingzhu's passing, the assembly wanted to appoint their head monk as the abbot of the temple. Jiufeng would not acknowledge him. He said, "Wait till I examine him. If he understands our late master's spirit and intention, I will serve him as I served our late master." So he gave the head monk some words of the late teacher and said, "Tell me, what sort of matter did he clarify with this?" The head monk said, "He clarified the matter of the One Color." Jiufeng said, "If so, you have not yet understood our late master's spirit."
>
> The head monk said, "Don't you acknowledge me? Pass me incense." He lit the incense and said, "If I had not understood our late master's spirit, I would not be able to pass away while the smoke of this incense rises." No sooner had he said this than he expired while sitting in meditation. Jiufeng caressed his back and said, "Dying while sitting or standing is not impossible. But you could not even dream of our late master's spirit."

Jiufeng determined that either the head monk had not seen emptiness or he actually had (the one color) but stayed in Zen sickness and hadn't moved on from nondual unity. Attached to emptiness, the head monk was furious that he was rejected and so petulantly died in protest to prove his supernatural powers. Other than being a phenomenally stupid thing to do (even if a metaphorical event), he could not even dream of his late master's spirit because he mistook the superpowers of self-induced death for realization. We can have amazing skills and still be deluded. Besides, concentration is not the aim of Zen, liberation is. That was his late master's intent.

This is why the poor are blessed and the Kingdom of heaven is theirs (saying 54). Those lacking conceptual walls and who have a poverty of notions about spiritual practice are free to be blessed with a wealth of wisdom. In case 10, "Qingshui the Poor" of the *Gateless Gate*, the monk Qingshui eagerly asked Master Caoshan Benji, "I am solitary and poor. I beg you master, please help me to become prosperous." Caoshan Benji said, "Venerable Qingshui!" "Yes master!" replied Qingshui. Caoshan Benji said, "You have already drunk three cups of fine Hakka wine and still you say that you have not yet moistened your lips."

In this koan Qingshui claims that he is "solitary and poor," meaning that he is a solitary one, an enlightened person. However, he has not fully realized nonduality since he asks for help, which shows that he still has concepts about gaining something. To gain something we must feel we lack something, but this is not the case in emptiness. Master Caoshan Benji's response demonstrates that Qingshui doesn't need to feel this way. The simple call and response is treasure in itself since it is emptiness and contains the whole universe. This koan demonstrates that those who are not rich in the type of mental obstructions that prevent entry into the Kingdom can be living ones. To be poor in this sense is positive.

To not overwhelm our senses with too many material possessions can also be considered advantageous. This is not support for the type of crushing poverty that robs people of dignity and life, since poverty and debt contribute to suffering in the world. Rather, it is talking about the kind of material simplicity that we voluntarily enter into and which does not induce suffering but acts as an aid to enlightenment. The *Song of Enlightenment* describes the link between this and spiritual wealth:

> Sons of the Sakya are known to be poor; But their poverty is of the body, their spiritual life knows no poverty. The poverty-stricken body is wrapped in rags, but their spirit holds within itself a rare invaluable gem.

Realization is the true treasure. So is the Kingdom. The *Comprehensive Treatise on the Mahayana* urges us to think of the inexhaustible wealth— spiritual and physical—stored in the dharmakaya. This sense of abundance means that contentment and happiness are not dependent upon material wealth but upon the heart-mind state of the solitary one.

Another Zen story illustrates the fact that contentment is not dependent upon material wealth. Zen Master Fugai Ekun once supported many student monks in his monastery. They were often too numerous to be supported by his insufficient funds. This really worried those disciples whose duty it was to look after the food supply. They didn't want to eat food that was cheaper but not as good quality.

One day a disciple advised the master not to admit new students anymore into the monastery. "We can't feed them," he said. Without replying the master lolled out his tongue and said: "Now look into my mouth, and tell me if there is any tongue in it." The perplexed disciple answered that there was. "Then don't bother yourself about it. If there is any tongue, I can taste any sort of food." In Zen honest poverty is considered one of the characteristics of an enlightened person.

Saying 4 states that if a person does not know themselves, they will live in poverty and will be poverty. If you do know yourself, it says, then you are wealthy and you are that wealth. If we move through saying 54, 63, and 78 respectively, contemplating the lessons of each one in turn, we arrive at an even more profound lesson than just saying 4 alone.

We find that when buddhas are truly buddhas they don't even perceive they are buddhas. Yet because they are enlightened they continue actualizing Buddhahood. In non-Zen speak this means that when we see the emptiness of the Kingdom we realize great wealth. If we cling to our knowledge of realization, however, then we are no different from other people. To be truly awakened we must move beyond knowing ourselves (saying 4) to truly live in the Kingdom of suchness. This is how we actualize our true nature.

When we fully integrate our insight into a natural way of living, we know that there is no enlightenment or delusion, and neither are there ignorant people or solitary ones. We continue to actualize and maintain our wisdom-being as Jesus does, as thusness itself. At last we know the answer to saying 11's crucial question: "When you come to dwell in the light, what will you do?"

34

SUFFERING

Blessed is the man who has suffered and found life.

—*Gospel of Thomas*, saying 58

A monk asked Tung Shan, "Cold and heat come. How can we avoid them?" Tung Shan said, "Why don't you go to the place where there is neither cold nor heat?" "What is the place where there is neither cold nor heat?" the monk asked. Tung Shan said, "When it's cold, kill yourself with cold. When it's hot, kill yourself with heat."

—*Blue Cliff Record*, case 43

Saying 58 gives us a method for dealing with suffering—use it to overcome it. In whatever way we encounter it, suffering can be the method by which we unfold our essential self and enter the Kingdom. We can liken this to the secret that Jesus told us about in John 16:32–33 when he said that in the world we will have dis-ease but we should be undaunted for, like him, we can overcome the world, too. It is not by escaping the world that we become a living one but by diving deep into it. It is possible to be in the world and overcome it at the same time.

There are a number of sayings in *Thomas* that deal with this theme. Saying 68 states that blessed is the person in the midst of persecution who, when they hate and pursue you even to the core of your being, cannot find "you" anywhere. When Jesus speaks of those of us in the midst of persecution, he is drawing our attention to the fact that anything that makes us suffer (as opposed to gives us pain) is something that challenges our ego. These can be used as teaching tools if we use them in a certain way.

A living one knows that ultimately there is no escape from reality purely because there is nothing outside of it to escape to. This means that we can't overcome our suffering by trying to escape from it. We must face it head-on. Both the Buddha and Jesus found freedom within suffering, not from it.

In case 43 of the *Blue Cliff Record* a monk asked Zen Master Dongshan Liangjie (referred to as Tung Shan in the translation above), "Cold and heat come. How can we avoid them?" Dongshan replied, "Why don't you go to the place where there is neither cold nor heat?" "What is the place where there is neither cold nor heat?" asked the monk. Dongshan explained, "When it's cold, kill yourself with cold. When it's hot, kill yourself with heat."

My late Dharma grandfather (my teacher's teacher) Master Koun Yamada taught that this koan is showing us there is no place where we do not feel heat or cold, but there is a place where we do not suffer from them: right smack in the middle of them. There is no way we can escape suffering, sadness, sickness, and death. This is the law of causality. But it is in the very midst of suffering that we escape suffering. There is no other way.

Finding liberation in the midst of suffering is the recognition of emptiness and another angle on suffering: even though there is persecution and hatred in the world that is directed at people, there is a place where no persecution takes place. This is the place where rejection does not reach—emptiness. It is the knowledge that it is not really suffering that goes away but the (separate) person who suffers. In other words, we recognize that the separation between ourselves and the ultimate is fiction. We don't own our suffering because there is no permanent, substantial, and separate "us." So rather than "our suffering" it is just suffering. This takes the bitter woe-is-me sting out of it.

In saying 69 Jesus says, "Blessed are those who are persecuted in their hearts. They are those who have known the Father in truth! Blessed are those who are hungry, because they will satisfy their bellies to their content!" When we actively seek for a way to end our suffering, we can find it. Saying 40 supports this and tells us that wisdom to see the Kingdom also ensures that anything planted outside the Father, being unsound, will be pulled up by its roots and destroyed.

Pulling up the roots of suffering and destroying them are another way to ensure that the house of self is never reconstructed. Our wisdom eye sees clearly that we are a part of a whole that is capable of wonderful transformation and love. Zen Master Eihei Dogen put it clearly in his text *Discourse on the Practice of the Way* when he said that "each and every thing is simply the One Mind from which nothing whatsoever is excluded."

Similarly, our negative proclivities are never set apart from Jesus because nothing is separate from the Kingdom. There is never complete and total severance from the Kingdom because that would be the same as nonbeing. It is all and in all, so anything other than that would lack ontological reality.

The fact that nothing is separate means that the kleshas are not infallible. In order not to have our hands bound by our own conceits, we can pull kleshas up by the roots. But if these roots are not cut, then the weed continues to grow because it has a contingent and causal relationship to us. If the cause is removed, then the suffering disappears, but if the cause is still present, so too is the problem.

The Buddha was once invited by a Brahmin, a member of the upper caste, to a meal. But when he arrived, the Brahmin greeted him rudely with a torrent of abuse. Politely, the Buddha asked, "Do visitors come to your home?" "Yes." "What preparations do you make for them?" "We get ready a great feast." "What happens if they don't arrive?" "Then we gladly eat it ourselves." "What happens if they don't accept the food?" "It becomes mine." "Well, Brahmin, you've invited me for a meal and you've entertained me with hard words. I want nothing from your preparation.

"So please take it back and eat it yourself. That with which you revile, scold and abuse me who has not done the same to you, I do not accept. It is yours. A person who reviles when reviled, abuses when abused and scolds when scolded—it is as if a host and a visitor dined together and made good. We, Brahmin, have not dined together nor made good. It is yours Brahmin. I give it back. It belongs to you." "Never retaliate in kind," the Buddha told his followers. "Hatred does not come to an end through hatred but can only end through nonhatred."

In this story the Brahmin is a metaphor for the kleshas of pride, arrogance, anger, conceit, false views, and moral shamelessness. The Buddha, representing wisdom itself, does not fall prey to those very same faults. Instead, he simply turns away and doesn't engage with them. Unlike the good man in saying 65, in his wisdom he has seen that to invest any time and energy into the kleshas is to invite disaster. "That which is not yours—put it away," the Buddha advised. "Putting it away will be to your welfare and happiness." If we see only the material, we think we own our perceptions, mental constructs, possessions, emotions, and body when in fact the owner, the master, is our true self.

Case 97, "Getting Despised" (also known as "The Diamond Cutter Scripture's Scornful Revilement") in the *Blue Cliff Record*, expresses the virtue of abuse. It states that the *Diamond Sutra* says: "If you are despised by others and are about to drop into hell because of your evil karma in your previous life, then because you are despised by others, the evil karma of your previous life will be extinguished."

There are two understandings of this. The first one is a literal interpretation, that bad karma can be extinguished in the here and now by virtue of the fact that abuse and scorn lead us to use appropriate and positive measures (such as the precepts) to overcome our suffering. Verses 3–5 of the *Dhammapada* express one such strategy. This is the recognition that people who harbor the thoughts "he abused me, he beat me, he defeated me, he robbed me," will never erase their hatred. "He abused me, he beat me, he defeated me, he robbed me—in those who do not harbor such thoughts hatred will cease. Hatred does not cease by hatred at any time: hatred ceases by non-hatred."

The *Song of Enlightenment* says that there is virtue in abusive words, and that the scandalmonger, for example, can be a good teacher. If we do not become angry at gossip, we have no need for powerful endurance under insult. If we learn useful strategies to alleviate suffering, then we don't need to be so defensive, reactive and prickly. Going to the root of our suffering and cutting off its food let it starve.

The second understanding of case 97 is the understanding of emptiness. As Jesus points out, a person is blessed if they suffer because they find their essential nature. When we do that, we also dissolve negative karma. This is because if we truly know the emptiness beyond absolution, we see that the real diamond in the *Diamond Sutra* is the jewel of our essential nature. Negative karma can operate only in an atmosphere of separateness, of self and other—of "me" doing this to "you" and vice versa. Self-centeredness always generates karma. Knowing or being essential unity allows us to embody nonharm because we act from an awareness of no one to be harmed and no one to do the harming. In this way suffering is either reduced or eliminated.

The fact that suffering itself is empty does not mean that we search out suffering or jump for joy when we suffer. What it means is that we come to see that encountering ego-threatening situations and people can be the way to realization. The *Song of Enlightenment* describes this when it says that some people slander and abuse others but in the end they are merely tiring themselves out. If we hear their scandal as though it were ambrosial truth, immediately everything melts and we enter the place beyond thought and words.

It is the nature of the world that there will always be people who do not, for whatever reason, give credit where credit is due. As the Buddha told us in the *Dhammapada*: "Indeed, this is an ancient practice, not one only of today: they blame those who remain silent, they blame those who speak much, they blame those who speak in moderation. There is none in the world who is not blamed for something." To be patient, keep our ordinary mind, and be unaffected by the disapproval of others is extremely hard to do but positive in its effect. As the *Sutra in Forty-Two Sections* makes clear, great power lies in patience under insult.

Buddha said: What is magnanimity, but the untiring exercise of patience under injury? He who bravely bears injury undeserved is a man indeed!

Those who are patient do not feed resentment. On the contrary it can be the impetus for resilience, strength, and peace.

When we struggle against reality rather than experiencing and accepting it, we add suffering to our pain. By virtue of the fact that we are human beings, suffering is inevitable at some point. We can't escape it. This is also why it is said in Buddhism that there is no nirvana except where the world of suffering is, and there is no world of suffering apart from nirvana. It is within the world and within our afflictions that we find release.

One way the Buddha found to accept suffering was by making a distinction between pain and suffering.

When a not-learned ordinary man feels unpleasant feelings he grieves, wearies, wails, beats the breast and comes to bewilderment of mind. He feels for two feelings bodily and mental. Like a man pricked by an arrow, he is pricked by a second arrow and feels two impacts. Touched by these unpleasant feelings he becomes resistant and averse, and as a result these latent tendencies stream to him. When touched by unpleasant feelings he then proceeds to enjoy sensory pleasures.

So what this is saying is that when we experience pain, we often add an extra psychological element to this.

This second element or dart is a tendency of rejection, resistance, and resentment. When we feel this, our natural instinct is to escape. So we then look for it in some sort of sensory gratification, whether that's alcohol, food, shopping, or drugs. Since we do not know of an effective way to deal with and accept pain, we often develop a tendency to habitually seek pleasant feelings whenever we experience unpleasant ones. No matter how natural this might be, it just masks the true situation because we don't deal with the root of the problem first.

A person who understands the role of suffering and how it differs from pain does not reject, resist, or resent what is happening to them, and so no secondary tendency (the second dart) is created. Instead, they accept the reality of pain and apply appropriate and skillful measures. The Buddha once had splinters in his feet, but while he felt pain, he did not suffer. There is a difference. There will always be pain, he said, but how you see it and deal with it is important to living a good life.

Sayings 40, 58, and 68 express the idea that suffering is not an impediment to enlightenment. Instead, it can be used to break the stranglehold of the ego and to transform ignorance into wisdom. Both Jesus and the Buddha took a constructive attitude toward suffering because it has the power to transform us. Suffering is the opportunity to train our heart-minds.

35

NONATTACHMENT

Jesus said, "I'll destroy [this] house, and no one will be able to build it [. . .]" again.

—*Gospel of Thomas*, saying 71

With the house demolished and the self overthrown, no inside or outside remains. So where, pray, are body and mind to conceal their forms?

—*Record of Transmitting the Light*, case 4

Saying 71 is based upon the theme of homelessness, the state in which a solitary one has left the house of the separate self for the homeless life of enlightenment. This way of life is not based on attachment to concepts and things. Rather than investing in the constricted and static separate self, the person in saying 71 is announcing that they have chosen the open, free-flowing, and spacious life of the true self instead.

To be completely free from the control of the self, the old "house" has to give way to a new mansion unlimited by time and space. Zen Master Eihei Dogen said that when we throw ourselves into the house of Buddha, the Dharma fills our hands. The *Mahaparinirvana Sutra* suggests that a fully aware person must live in the house of enlightenment, and they should use the house for its real purpose, not for a selfish one.

This requires nothing less than the death of the separate self, the house builder of saying 71.

The end result of entrance into the Kingdom is the destruction of both the house (the ego) and the house builder (the separate self) so that nothing like them can ever be built again. In describing his enlightenment experience in the *Dhammapada*, the Buddha said, "O housebuilder, you are seen! You will not build this house again. For your rafters are broken and your ridgepole shattered. My mind has reached the unconditioned."

The rafters of this self-created house are the kleshas—attachment, aversion, illusion, conceit, false views, doubt, apathy, restlessness, and moral shamelessness. The ridgepole supporting these is ignorance (of the true nature of the Kingdom). It is wisdom that shatters this house of separate self so that the ego-based building materials (kleshas) can never be used again.

Chapter 4 of the *Record of Transmitting the Light* tells us that the Venerable Shonawashu once asked the monk Ubakikuta prior to his enlightenment whether it was his body or mind that renounced this world and became a monk. This is a checking question to see if Ubakikuta sees emptiness or separation. Ubakikuta replies, "In fact, it was my body." The Venerable Shonawashu then says, "How could the wonderful Dharma of all buddhas have anything to do with body or mind?" Thereupon the monk came to a great enlightenment. Shonawashu was pointing out that there is no separate self or separate body to be enlightened. Everything is enlightened in the essential world because of its very nature. This is why Master Keizan's appreciatory verse says: "With the house demolished and the self overthrown, no inside or outside remains. So where, pray, are body and mind to conceal their forms?"

Another way of saying this is saying 42: "Become passersby." Sometimes translated as "be transients" or "be itinerants," it is also saying that nonattachment is a must for anyone who wants to live a good life. As *Dhammapada* 91 suggests, "the thoughtful exert themselves; they do not delight in a home. Like swans who have left their lake, they leave their house and home."

They know that in emptiness there is no landlord to pay rent to. Besides, they have invested in something worth more than any mortgage—the true self. This leaves them free to partake of movement and repose whenever they want. Like birds they fly free.

Other translations of this saying are "come into being as you pass away" and "become yourselves while passing away." As the separate self dies, our true self comes into light. Someone who has seen the unseen no longer lives a life that revolves around wants and desires because their lives don't revolve around the separate self. Freedom involves passing by the lure not only of material things but also of the self. If there is no separate self, who and what are there to attach to?

This freedom doesn't mean that material things are not important, but just that they are not the *most* important. When someone lives with a well-developed awareness of the empty nature of the world, they are also free to put down and pick up at will. This cannot happen if we are attached to things. This is why saying 71 is warning us that attachment should be discarded because it causes suffering.

As I mentioned before, desire is often mistakenly identified in Buddhism as the sole cause of suffering, so it's best to be flexible in how we interpret it. Sometimes the Buddha spoke of desire itself (to be in a state of want) as the cause of suffering, but at other times he also meant negative desire (as in the desire to kill or hurt), as well as attachment, neediness, and craving. All of these words describe the situation in which we attempt to hold on to what cannot be held. We either want things to become permanent—to escape from what we dislike—or we want to take ourselves out of the system.

It would be a pity, then, if we did to passersby what was done to detachment by European intellectuals in the nineteenth century. British and German scholars painted a particular view of Buddhism that unfortunately still lingers today. They spread the mistaken impression that detachment meant a dry and unfeeling way of life that was essentially escapist and inward looking. The popular image became the solitary individual completely disconnected from the concerns of the world. Nothing could be further from the truth.

Detachment is an unfortunate and rigid expression that carries a tone of intellectual remoteness. Unfortunately, many people today still use it rather than *nonattachment* to describe the state in which we are no longer under the sway of greed, anger, and ignorance. Yet enlightenment is not cold and uncaring. Quite the opposite. *Nonattachment*, the term I prefer, is characterized by joy, equanimity, loving-kindness, and compassion.

Sayings 71 and 42 do not promote the idea that homelessness means retreating from the world. Instead, they corroborate Jesus in John 8:32 when he said, "And you shall know the truth and the truth shall make you free." As we say in Zen: "The Way is intrinsically accomplished; The principle of Zen is complete freedom." Boundless freedom and not cold detachment is one and the same with the realization of the truth. To become passersby is to be liberated. This is what happens when we become our true selves as we pass away.

36

KENSHO

The Kingdom of the father is like a certain woman who was carrying a jar full of meal. While she was walking on the road, still some distance from home, the handle of the jar broke and the meal emptied out behind her on the road. She did not realize it; she had noticed no accident. When she reached her house, she set the jar down and found it empty.

—*Gospel of Thomas*, saying 97

In this way and that I tried to save the old pail
Since the bamboo strip was weakening and about to break
Until at last the bottom fell out.
No more water in the pail!
No more moon in the water!
Emptiness in my hand!

—*Zen Flesh, Zen Bones*, Chiyono and the Pail

A surface interpretation of saying 97 gives us the impression that this saying is about a careless and mindless woman who has a serious case of forgetfulness. She has such a lack of attentiveness that she doesn't even know that the contents of her jar have leaked out onto the road. Only when she gets home does she realize something is wrong. Scratch just a bit beneath this however, and we find a description of kensho, an enlightenment event.

The experience of the woman in saying 97 is known in Zen as the great death. This is the death of the separate self and also what Zen Buddhists refer to as "kicking through the bottom of the bucket." This expression refers to the story of the Buddhist nun Mugai Nyodai (also known by her childhood name Chiyono) who practiced Zen for years but was unable to find enlightenment. One moonlit night she was carrying an old bucket filled with water. She was watching the full moon reflected in this water when the bamboo strip that held the bucket broke. It fell into pieces, the water rushed out, the moon's reflection disappeared and Chiyono found emptiness.

This sudden liberation obviously came after a struggle with trying to keep it all together: "I tried to save the old pail since the bamboo strip was weakening and about to break." Like most of us, Chiyono tried her best to keep the various ego-based parts of her self in working order, keeping up appearances and reinforcing the walls. The irony in this is that it takes so much energy not to spill over our self-made boundaries.

But when, like Chiyono, we discover who we truly are—that the ground of being is bottomless—we realize that no matter how much we put into the bucket, it is never filled. Yet it contains everything! This great death (of separate self) results in great life. As case 5 of the *Gateless Gate* tells us: "If you can respond to it (essential nature) fittingly, you will give life to those who have been dead, and put to death those who have been alive."

The fact that she did not know the jar was empty is considered a good kind of unknowing in Zen. Ironically the "don't-know" mind is considered a sign of realization. Knowing something usually means having a lot of facts in our head about something. But in saying 97 the woman did not accumulate concepts and intellectual knowledge that would entail separation between the person who is doing the knowing and the thing to know. Instead, she had moved beyond the knower and the known into the unity of emptiness.

Saying 97 and Chiyono's poem are also descriptions of two different types of enlightenment experiences—gentle and sudden kensho, a breakthrough process or event in which a person glimpses emptiness. It is not enlightenment but rather an enlightenment event. My teacher, Seiun An Roshi of the Mountain Moon Zen Society, likens it to a scratch on a dirty window. We have not instantly become a mystical Zen master who sees and knows all; we've just discovered that there's a bigger picture we never knew existed before. Kensho is just the beginning of our journey into the Kingdom.

So enlightenment is not kensho. Kensho is a moment of insight and not an end in itself. The woman in saying 97 has put in effort to be at this point, and she must continue to work on this till it grows into a deeply mature and practical wisdom. Enlightenment is wisdom refined through lived experience, meditation, and study.

As for sudden and gentle awakenings to emptiness, both of these occur in Zen too. Many times a practitioner will have a combination of the two, since prolonged koan practice gradually opens us to reality and a sudden moment of insight perforates the last bit of resistance we have.

It is considered bad form (and an ego trip) in some Zen circles to talk about our own kensho experience. I was told by my teacher to completely forget about it and not mention it to anyone. This was so I wouldn't attach to it as some "thing" to obtain. So perhaps these sorts of conventions in Zen have meant that there's not much talk about the fact that kensho takes all forms and shapes. Like any mystical experience, kensho is pretty darn hard to describe anyway.

The stereotypical image of a kensho event is of a person who experiences a sudden and intense sense of freedom and release from the self. They might spend a long time in the clouds just enjoying their discovery before they come back to the ground. This certainly seems like Chiyono's experience. The woman in saying 97 however, had a different encounter.

She did not realize that she had broken the shell of the separate self. Over time she had not noticed that the ego was gradually being worn away. So "when she reached her house, she set the jar down and found it empty." This is a way of saying that, as the culmination of practice, one day she thought to herself—"Oh yeah, that's right, it's all empty. I knew that."

Koun Yamada Roshi once spoke to a woman in the United States who had had a certain experience that she didn't seem to think was very important because it was a gentle experience of insight, like the turning of a page in a book. After questioning her about this experience the roshi confirmed that she did in fact experience kensho. So sometimes we are like the woman with the jar—emptiness rolls in one day and touches us softly on the shoulder.

Sutta Nipata 3.8 states that just as all earthen vessels made by the potter end in being broken, so is the life of mortals. Like saying 97, the surface meaning relates to the phenomenal world—we all break apart at some stage. The deeper meaning is that we are empty. When we discover this, the shell of the self breaks apart. This is something all of us can do. Whether we learn the lessons of impermanence and emptiness in a sudden or a gradual way is irrelevant. What is important is that we continue to take one step after the other just like the woman in saying 97 and Mugai Nyodai, the first female Zen master.

37

THE KOAN OF NOT-WORTHY

Simon Peter said to them, "Let Mariham go out from among us, for women are not worthy of the life." Jesus said, "Look, I will lead her that I may make her male, in order that she too may become a living spirit resembling you males. For every woman who makes herself male will enter into the Kingdom of heaven."

—*Gospel of Thomas*, saying 114

Once in the ancient days of the World-Honored One, Manjushri went to the place where buddhas were assembled and found that all the buddhas were departing for their original dwelling places. Only a young woman remained, sitting in samadhi close to Shakyamuni Buddha's throne. Manjushri asked the Buddha, "Why can that woman be near the Buddha's throne while I cannot?" The Buddha said, "Just awaken her and raise her up out of samadhi and ask her yourself." Manjushri walked around the woman three times, snapped his fingers once, took her up to the Brahman heaven, and exerted all his supernatural powers, but he could not bring her out of samadhi. The World-Honored One said, "Even a hundred or a thousand Manjushris would not be able to bring her out of samadhi."

—*Gateless Gate*, case 42

At first glance saying 114 is a sucker punch. Some translations use the words "not worthy of the life" (meaning religious life) while others go even further and announce that "women are not worthy of life." Either way the reader of *Thomas* is led through an intriguing corridor only to have the door shut on a particular group when they reach the end. I hung my head when I first read this.

Since I am a twenty-first-century woman, along the way I forgave the few things about females in the *Gospel of Thomas* that were not so positive (reasoning that all texts are products of a historical context), and I was encouraged by some aspects of male-female transcendence. But then I was deeply and suddenly disappointed by the words at the end—that you don't make the grade as you are. My immediate reaction was a series of questions. Does this rule out everything that came before? What parts do I now believe? Was saying 22 just for show? What is the deeper meaning?

If saying 114 causes consternation, as I'm sure it does for some, one way of responding to it is to take it in the manner that a student took the blows of a Zen master in ancient China. Some koans describe Zen masters hitting students with their *nyoi* (a short stick representing authorization as a master). The teacher would use such a method not to punish or cause injury, but to instantly stop discursive thinking, and to jolt a student into a mode more favorable to enlightenment. Saying 114 can be just such a hit.

The koan "not worthy" can be used as an impetus to question our own egos as a determinant of reaction, to contemplate meanings not immediately apparent, and to let buddha nature solve all conundrums, if even to say that "not worthy" cannot be reconciled in the end with our own experience of emptiness. Moreover, a reading of the *Lotus Sutra*, which contains parallels to saying 114, both in text and controversy, can help shed some light as well.

The *Lotus Sutra* is one of the most popular and influential texts in Mahayana Buddhism and the central text used by the Tendai and

Nichiren sects. Influential in the lives of at least three Zen masters (Hakuin Ekaku, Daijian Huineng, and Eihei Dogen), it is also important in Zen, with Master Dogen referring to it as the "sutra of sutras." As an early Mahayana sutra it is considered both a prototype and a complete representation of the heart and culmination of the Buddha's teaching, and for this reason it is very highly regarded by Mahayana Buddhists in East Asia.

If we look at the egalitarian aspect of the sutra, it clearly states that everyone, including women, can attain enlightenment. Naturally it has enjoyed popularity with women because of this. This idea was not new, however. The Buddha himself said that women were equally capable of realization, and as a consequence, he approved a female monastic order. This was a radical experiment. When a daughter was born to his friend, King Pasenadi, he reassured him that it was just as joyous an occasion as the birth of a boy. "A woman might turn out better than a man," he said.

The problem in the *Lotus Sutra*, as in most cases of Buddhist sutras suggesting the equality of women, is that there is a requirement attached that is not present for men. So, for example, the Buddha created a monastic order for women but gave a number of extra rules to govern their behavior, as well as subordinating them to monks. Additionally, suggestions of the positive capacities of women are often paired with those that suggest the exact opposite.

So while a woman "may turn out better than a man," some Buddhist texts also suggest the complete opposite. For instance, the predicted consequence of the ordination of women was that Buddhism would simply die out. While it has been argued that this was a later addition inserted into the text, statements such as this have tended to negate or diminish any positive ones about women.

Five examples in the *Lotus Sutra* clearly exemplify the above, and illustrate the tensions between women as impure and women as wisdom itself. In terms of presenting completely opposite messages, in chapter 23 of the *Lotus Sutra* it is proclaimed that if a woman who hears the chapter and accepts and upholds it, it will be her last appearance in a woman's body. To be born in the form of a man is a reward for hearing the wisdom of the sutra.

Yet in chapter 14 of the sutra the Buddha advises that we should not make distinctions by saying "this is a woman" or "this is a man," since an awakened person finds that all things are "not produced, void, immovable, everlasting; this is called the proper sphere of the wise." This suggests that emptiness has no gender, and that gender is not a determinant of realization.

In terms of caveats added to the ability of women, in chapter 1 of the sutra a great assembly is gathered to hear the Buddha preach the *Lotus Sutra*. The fact that the Buddha's wife and aunt, Mahaprajapati and Yasodhara, are present can be seen as evidence of a positive attitude toward women. However, despite the fact that their followers in the crowd number in the thousands, these two are the only women actually named. The rest remain anonymous, and it is unclear what their status is.

This seems to be a compromise between societal attitudes and the recognition of universal buddha nature. In other words, the writers of the sutra could only refer to women indirectly and symbolically through Mahaprajapati and Yasodhara. There is a definite reluctance in the sutra to discuss these two women in as much depth as the men, other than to say that they must work harder at realization than them.

In chapter 13 both of these women receive a prophecy from the Buddha of their eventual buddhahood. They look at him questioningly. The Buddha tells Mahaprajapati not to be perplexed since she will eventually "be a Bodhisattva and preacher of the law [Dharma] . . . under the name of Sarvasattvapriyadarsana [Lovely to See for All Beings], a Tathagata [Buddha], an Arhat [a perfected person] . . . endowed with science and conduct." Similarly, Yasodhara will also become a bodhisattva and preacher of the law.

The good news, then, is that both of them will have many followers and become great teachers of the Dharma. This is clear proof of the universality of buddha nature. Yet the conditions under which they become teachers also illustrate certain attitudes about the inability of women to achieve enlightenment in the same manner as men. While the *Lotus Sutra* states that enlightenment can occur within a lifetime, indeed within an instant of insight, the conditions placed upon Mahaprajapati and Yasodhara suggest women are not capable of that.

This is because they only receive enlightenment after many lifetimes of practice and after going through various stages, which the *Lotus Sutra* suggests are not necessary if one has faith. There are no other places in the sutra where the various stages required to attain enlightenment are so completely detailed.

It seems plausible, then, that this is attributable to the common view of the hindrances presented by the female body. The female body was seen as a symbol of attachment to the world. In fact, one reason why monasticism and celibacy were recommended for women was that it prevented two key impediments to enlightenment—intercourse and the birth of children—from coming into play.

Since these would no longer occur, it is easy to see why, in effect, this was perceived as transforming the female body into that of a male, and repudiating the female nature. Since strict fasting would eventually prevent menstruation, women would no longer defile themselves through their own sexual desires and feminine bodily processes. Rather, they would become "male" through the solitary life, and through the insight that would bring about an enlightened (male) state. In the *Sakkapanna Suttanta*, for example, Gopika entered a state of enlightenment after she abandoned a woman's mentality and cultivated a "man's mentality."

It could be argued, then, that transforming the female body into that of a male can be interpreted in two ways. The change from "female" to "male" is a metaphoric one; that women turn from a preoccupation with sense gratification to a concern for religious realization. This would apply to men as well. In this sense, "male" and "female" are merely designations for states of mind. This line of thinking is prominent among apologists and those who wish to interpret the sutras from an essential viewpoint that does not discriminate in terms of gender.

This has certainly been the interpretation not only for the *Lotus Sutra* but many other texts in addition to those already mentioned. In the thirty-fifth *Vow of Amida Buddha*, for example, Amida Buddha, the celestial and principal buddha in Pure Land Buddhism, pledges the following:

> If, after I have obtained enlightenment, women in immeasurable, innumerable, inconceivable, incomparable, immense Buddha countries on all sides, after having heard my name, should allow carelessness to arise, should not turn their thoughts toward enlightenment, should, when they are free from birth, not despise their female nature; and if they, being born again, should assume a second female nature, then may I not obtain the highest perfect knowledge.

This can be seen as a vow not to become fully enlightened until all people, regardless of gender, become enlightened and move from a "female" state of mind to a realized "male" consciousness. Seen in this light, this is a selfless bodhisattva vow.

On the other hand, however, this may suggest that women must become men through rebirth (an actual physical change) and thereby repudiate completely their female nature. The implication here is that, despite the Buddha stating that realization is for all, enlightenment is often expressed, either metaphorically or physically, in purely male terms.

The famous story of the *naga* (dragon) girl in the *Lotus Sutra* illustrates how it is possible to have multiple interpretations of this transformation of gender. In chapter 12, we are given evidence of instantaneous enlightenment when an eight-year-old naga princess hears the *Lotus Sutra*. When she announces her prowess in the Dharma and that she can attain enlightenment, Shariputra expresses his doubt and derision.

Shariputra was one of the two chief male disciples of the Buddha and had a reputation as the person "foremost in wisdom." He expressed his disbelief by saying to the naga girl:

> It may happen, sister, that a woman displays an unflagging energy, performs good works for many thousands of eons, and fulfils the six perfect virtues, but as yet there is no example of her having reached Buddhaship, and that is because a woman cannot occupy the five ranks, viz. 1. the rank of Brahma; 2. the rank of Indra; 3. the rank of a chief guardian of the four quarters; 4. the rank of Cakravartin; 5. the rank of a Bodhisattva incapable of sliding back.

The five hindrances he is referring to are the five capabilities (listed above) that women were said not to possess. Since in some sects of Mahayana Buddhism it is held that through good deeds and realized insight anyone can enter the god or buddha realm (two of the worlds we can be reborn or incarnated in), the inability to become either a god-king or a buddha is a direct refutation of that belief.

The naga girl, however, proves him wrong by becoming enlightened. She does this by changing to a man in the space of an instant, going to another world in another dimension, sitting on a jeweled lotus blossom, and instantly attaining enlightenment. Once done, she returns as a woman. It is said that all the assembled multitude, including Shariputra, "silently believed and accepted."

What are we to make of this? On one hand this is a slap on the wrist for the arrogant Shariputra and direct proof that he is wrong. In fact, it is the only case in the whole of Buddhist literature where any mortal instantly becomes a buddha. It is the good-news story of the sutra and evidence of the fact that there are no differences between genders in terms of ability.

So the change into a male is merely for show. The dragon girl is turning the tables on Shariputra by becoming like him and then not him, and thus overcoming the two genders altogether. She is showing him that male and female are just conventional terms. They are empty and have no self-nature of their own. Seen in this light, it is irrelevant whether a male changed into a female or a female into a male. It is simply an illustration of the nature of emptiness and oneness. It is also a positive demonstration that we can "attain buddhahood in this very body" and that this possibility is open to anyone. Kudos can be awarded to the princess for demonstrating the truth of the Dharma.

Yet—and there is almost always a "yet" in Buddhist texts—if indeed it was unimportant for a woman to change into a man, then why do it? Moreover, why are there no examples of men changing into women, except when it is done against their will as in the *Vimalakirti Nirdesa Sutra*? In this sutra a goddess employed her magical power to cause the elder Shariputra to appear in her form and to cause herself to appear in his form. While this change occurred to Shariputra to make him realize his attachments, it was still a matter of force, and a very rare example.

It's understandable that some Buddhists object to the fact that the dragon girl does not become a buddha in her female form. However, it has been suggested that we not only consider the psychology of the Indian people at this time, but that we do not let this detract from the point at hand—that through having a girl change into a man and become enlightened, the congregation was greatly impressed, more so than if it had been a man.

If we look at it in this light, sudden transformation of a woman into a man means nothing but the transcendence of the difference between male and female. Emptiness includes but also transcends gender, and female-male transformation was a way of using the cultural mores of the time to demonstrate a teaching point. Yet we still cannot ignore the fact that, if the idea of sexual transformation is in fact redundant (because there is no ultimate difference and women can attain enlightenment as women), then why is it present in sutras in the first place anyway?

Like saying 114, the *Lotus Sutra* is a conundrum. On one hand, it is clear from the sutra that women can not only achieve enlightenment but are capable of being great teachers as well. It is also clear that to be in a realized state is to reach the highest wisdom that sees the essential equality of all things. It is to lose attachment to gender because in the ultimate scheme of things it disappears in emptiness. The predictions of buddhahood for women and the demonstrations of that are clear proof that being a woman is not an impediment to enlightenment.

On the other hand, however, there are clear instances of gender bias. It is impossible to ignore the inferences of inferiority in the sutra toward the weakness of the female nature and body, and the one-way transformation given as the precondition for realization for women. To become enlightened, it is suggested, one must become male. There are certainly instances in the Buddhist canon that suggest that male and female become each other (in the sense that differences disappear in emptiness). In other words, an equal mutuality exists in this sense, but it is never exclusively suggested that the male must become the female in order for realization to occur. This one-way transformation implies a cultural, historical, and religious bias against women as the ideal representation of an enlightened person.

If we position saying 114 in light of all of the above, the same conclusion can be applied. While it can be argued that sayings such as saying 22 are also biased, that particular saying lends itself more to the mutuality of male and female in oneness than saying 114, which suggests wisdom is a one-way gender street. To instantly rule saying 114 out as completely misogynistic therefore is untenable since in light of the context of whole text, it is clear that Jesus is teaching both the emptiness of gender and the use of the "male" as a metaphorical representation of the realized state. On the other hand, it would be naive to think that, given the context of the time in which it was written, the female becoming the male is completely without bias.

At this point it might be helpful, however, to consider the notion that Jesus's use of the phrase "you males" suggests that he is speaking from a realized viewpoint, perhaps as an expedient means to alert the men to the implications of their attachment to their own conceptions. So it might be the case that this phrase was purposefully included in *Thomas* specifically as a teaching point about attachment to fixed categories. This could be another angle with which to view the inclusion of saying 114 in the gospel.

It is possible therefore, to use it in a manner similar to case 42, "A Woman Comes Out of Samadhi" of the *Blue Cliff Record*. In this case Manjushri is alarmed by the presence of a woman sitting near the Buddha. He tries to snap her out of meditation but can't do it.

> The World-Honored One then said, "Down below, past twelve hundred million lands as innumerable as the sand of the Ganges, is the Bodhisattva Moumyou. He will be able to arouse her from her samadhi." Instantly the Bodhisattva Moumyou emerged out of the earth and made a bow to the World-Honored One, who then gave his command. The Bodhisattva went before the woman and snapped his fingers once. At this, the woman came out of samadhi.

So here we have Manjushri, the symbol of *prajna* (the wisdom of the essential world), unable to understand why a woman (and a young girl at that) can be near an honored place and person when he, an enlightened male, cannot. To add insult to injury the Buddha tells him to ask the woman to come out of her meditative trance and he cannot do it! He tells him even a hundred or a thousand Manjushris would not be able to bring her out of *samadhi* (meditative absorption). Does the woman know something he does not and possess some power he doesn't have? One would think that Manjushri, a teacher of the Buddha himself and a person who has realized essential wisdom, would know most things. Yet he cannot do this simple task.

In the end it is Moumyou who arises from the earth, a symbol of groundedness and naturalness, and springs into action with a skillful and appropriate response. Despite the fact that Moumyou is a beginner (and a symbol of the phenomenal world in this koan) he holds no preconceived idea of what an enlightened person is. In this situation the fact that he is not advanced, and has not seen the essential, works in his favor. He just sees a person in meditative concentration and awakens her out of it. He knows the practical truths of the world.

Manjushri, on the other hand, clings to his own enlightenment and makes an idol and an object out of it. That object prevents him from acting freely and appropriately. While he is the symbol of the essential side of things and lives in emptiness where there is no coming and going, leaving (meditative absorption) and entering (another state), near or far from the Buddha, he lacks upaya because he stays in the world of emptiness and, as such, is ineffective in the phenomenal world. This is a reminder that we may know the secrets of the ultimate but still not know how to drive a car. The two truths of reality must be known for us to be a fully functioning individual.

As I have explained before, the middle way includes and is beyond both essential and phenomenal in a one-world, one-level reality. Due to this, Manjushri comes off second best in this particular situation. He knows much but cannot apply it usefully. His one-dimensional view causes him angst.

So perhaps Jesus was trying to shake these men out of the idolatry of their own "male" states of wisdom. They know the secrets of Jesus's teachings, but what is the use of that knowledge if they can't apply it well in ordinary situations? If they are severely distracted from the path just by the presence of women, then perhaps they need to contemplate the teachings some more. Perhaps they need to come down to earth.

Perhaps, in fact, they have not realized Jesus's wisdom teachings at all and are stuck in fixed categories of judgment.

Seen in this kind of light, the koan "not worthy" spurs me on to take *Thomas* at its word—that we must discern the truth of things for ourselves. Both Jesus and the Buddha were people of their time, and they applied their insights in ways adaptable and meaningful to the people of their era. So too should we learn the lessons of bias from saying 114 and seek to apply insights that are meaningful to our world and our lives today.

Applying these lessons is especially challenging for those Buddhists who feel that teachings are permanent and unchanging because the Buddha or a respected teacher taught them. For Buddhists who hold this opinion, what the Buddha said was unmediated and definitive. If this were not so, then anyone, even those without the clarity and insight of the Buddha, could claim anything they want. Some Christians might also feel that Jesus cannot say anything new and that teachings are fixed for all time. It is tempting to drift into doubt because the implication of this is that the Buddha (or Jesus) might himself have been wrong or sexist or unwilling to liberate women by changing tradition.

This doubt also applies to recognition of the fact that, while text is a reflection of a teacher's self-actualized knowledge, every teacher, even the Buddha, was a person of their own time. This means that traditional text may reflect social customs and attitudes that are no longer in existence. In weighing up saying 114, the tension between these facts must be acknowledged.

Yet ambivalence is not necessarily a bad thing. When things do not rest well with us, we can sit with that feeling of indecision. The meditative mind can hold all opposites at once. What this means is that it is entirely probable that there are no clear answers about the meaning of "not worthy." So our choices might be that we can be either comfortable with uncertainty or patiently wait until an answer arises from insight.

In this sense Buddhists are fortunate because we have an official religious disclaimer—we are allowed to and even encouraged to question the source of our information and to find the answers ourselves. The Buddha acquired the authority to spread the Dharma because he discovered the truth of the universe for himself. This is the same discovery he asks us to make. Authenticity in Buddhism (as in other wisdom traditions) depends not upon unquestioning belief in the teachings and scriptures, but upon individual and experiential discovery of their eternal truths. This is no different for the *Gospel of Thomas*.

This is what this koan is about—authenticity. If authenticity is a feature of true realization, then I must enact saying 114 in my own way, and that accords with both my own insight and the wisdom tradition handed down to me through my own Zen lineage. This means that I cannot in all good conscience embody the idea that I must become male if that involves any rejection of my female nature (in whatever way I may conceive of that). Neither will I seek to hide the bias of any text because I am either embarrassed or doubtful as to why that bias exists. It is no use denying the conundrums of historical discourse.

Consequently, while the wording of saying 114 will never sit well with me, and I recognize its inherent bias, it can still be used as skillful means either in a metaphorical sense (it suggests we must move from a mind attached to sense gratification to a unified oneness) or a soteriological one, that is, its own inherent bias confirms the liberating power of the Dharma.

Just by virtue of what it is, it can engender not only inappropriate responses but appropriate ones as well. For some it may be confirmation of the inherent inferiority of women, but for others it can provoke a sense of justice and equality. My reaction to saying 114 confirms to me that the correct way of viewing gender should be without attachment and in light of the essential genderless nature of the ultimate. I must trust my judgment on this.

There is room for both negative and exclusive, as well as positive and inclusive, readings of saying 114. What is important, then, is that we become a living one who, like Jesus, is aware of differences but has moved beyond a world completely encapsulated by them. This awareness reflects the true nature of the ultimate and the middle way and is a guide for all of us on the path.

Bibliography

Arnold, Kenneth. "The Circle of the Way: Reading the Gospel of Thomas as a Christian Text." *Cross Currents* 51 (2000): 459–469.

Bauman, Lynn. *The Gospel of Thomas: Wisdom of the Twin.* Ashland, Ore.: White Cloud Press, 2012.

Blatz, Beate. "The Coptic Gospel of Thomas." In *New Testament Apocrypha, Vol. 1: Gospels and Related Writings,* edited by W. Schneemelcher, translated by R. McL. Wilson, 110–134, Louisville, Ky.: Westminster/ John Knox Press, 1991.

Bourgeault, Cynthia. *The Wisdom Jesus: Transforming Heart and Mind: A New Perspective on Christ and His Message.* Boston: Shambhala Publications, 2011.

Davies, Stevan L. *The Gospel of Thomas and Christian Wisdom.* New York: Seabury Press, 1983.

Foulk, T. Griffith. "The Form and Function of Koan Literature: A Historical Overview." In *The Koan: Texts and Contexts in Zen Buddhism,* edited by Steven Heine and Dale S. Wright, 15–46, New York: Oxford University Press, 2000.

The Gospel of Thomas, translated by Thomas O. Lambdin. In *The Nag Hammadi Library in English,* edited by James. M. Robinson, 124–138, Leiden, the Netherlands: Brill, 1996.

The Gospel of Thomas Collection, The Gnostic Society Library. Accessed October 2016. http://gnosis.org/naghamm/nhl_thomas.htm.

Hori, Victor Sogen. *Zen Sand: The Book of Capping Phrases for Koan Practice.* Honolulu, Hawaii: Nanzan Library of Asian Religion and Culture, 2010.

The Koan: Texts and Contexts in Zen Buddhism. Edited by Steven Heine and Dale S. Wright, New York: Oxford University Press, 2000.

Leloup, Jean-Yves. *The Gospel of Thomas: The Gnostic Wisdom of Jesus.* Translated by Joseph Rowe. Rochester, Vt.: Inner Traditions, 2005.

Pagels, Elaine. *Beyond Belief: The Secret Gospel of Thomas.* New York: Vintage, 2004.

Patterson, Stephen J., and James M. Robinson. "The Gospel of Thomas." In *The Complete Gospels: Annotated Scholars Version,* edited by Robert J. Miller, 301–324, Farmington, Minn.: Polebridge Press, 1994.

Reps, Paul, and Nyogen Zenzaki. *Zen Flesh, Zen Bones.* Boston: Shambhala, 1994.

Suzuki, Daisetzu Teitaro. *The Zen Koan as a Means of Attaining Enlightenment.* Tokyo: Tuttle, 1994.

Valantasis, Richard. *The Gospel of Thomas.* London: Routledge, 1997.

INDEX

and wholeness, 50
nonseparation. *See* interconnection/
    nonseparation
"not born of woman" phrase, 99
"not worthy" koan, 210, 220
"nothing to drink" metaphor, 84
the now, the present (timelessness). *See
    also* children, infants
    experiencing, as basis for enlighten-
        ment, 39, 92
    living in, infants as models for, 10
    living in, and spiritual insight, xii,
        43–44, 59–61
    and opportunity, 60
    parinirvana (death) in, 92
nyoi stick (Zen Buddhism), 210

O

oak tree metaphor, 14
oneness. *See* interconnection/non-
    separation; nondual awareness/
    nonattachment
the other
    bowing to, as act of recognition, 101
    concern for the well-being of, 133–35
    loving as oneself, and the golden rule,
        139–41
    meeting as oneself, 97
    and sense of separateness, 129

P

pain vs. suffering, 198–99
Pajjota Sutta, on Buddha light, 154
Pali Canon, plowman metaphor, 56
paramitas (perfections), listing of, 172
parents. *See also* the father (the sole
    cause); the mother
    nondual perspective, 145–46, 149–50
    traditional perspective, 148–49
parinirvana (death), 92. *See also*
    deathlessness
Pathama Migajala Sutta, on the "lone
    dweller," 105, 107–8
patience, 114, 135, 172, 198
Paul, on being both a part of and the
    whole of the body of Christ, 125
pearl metaphor, 55

persecution, as a spiritual challenge,
    193–94
persimmon metaphor, 183–84
Peter, on Jesus as an external messiah, 75
Pharisees
    selfishness, 171
    stinginess, ignorance and denial of
        true wisdom by, 169–71
phenomenal/physical existence. *See also*
    nondual awareness/nonattachment;
    wholeness, non-separation
    breaking free from, 129–31
    and embracing, incorporating the
        spiritual, 177–78
    and gender distinctions, 123
    and limited vision, 122
    as part of the whole, 99–100, 158
philosophical concepts, 76
piety, outward displays of, 21–22
Platform Sutra
    and continuous nature of synthesis/
        integration, 80
    on the delusion of purity, 22–23
    on judgmentalism, 138
poverty, material simplicity, 189
practice approaches. *See* spiritual
    growth/practice
*Prajna Paramita Sutra on the Buddha-
    Mother's Producing the Three Dharma
    Treasures*, on mother wisdom, 149
prayer, ritual observance. *See also* spiri-
    tual growth/practice
    as empty actions, 21–22
    as manifestation of ego, 24
    prayerful hands, 101
    putting in proper context, 24
present moment. *See* children, infants;
    the now, the present
Proverbs 15:23, on timely speech, 173
Psalms 96:11, and the freedom and joy
    of enlightenment, 86–87
purity, delusion of
    admonitions against, 21–22
    and being true to one's essence, 105
    moving beyond, 22–24

ABOUT THE AUTHOR

 JOANNE P. MILLER was brought up in the Protestant tradition and belongs to the Mountain Moon Zen Society, a meditative community in the Sanbo-Zen tradition. Her books include *Buddhist Meditation and the Internet: Practices and Possibilities* and *Julian and the Buddha: Common Points Along the Way*. She has a PhD in the sociology of religion with qualifications in systematic theology and Buddhist studies. Her interests lie in the Buddhist and Christian mystical traditions, and the ways in which mystical insight can be applied to everyday life. She is currently teaching study of religion, philosophy and reason, history and English to senior high school students.

About Wisdom Publications

Wisdom Publications is the leading publisher of classic and contemporary Buddhist books and practical works on mindfulness. To learn more about us or to explore our other books, please visit our website at wisdompubs.org or contact us at the address below.

Wisdom Publications
199 Elm Street
Somerville, MA 02144 USA

We are a 501(c)(3) organization, and donations in support of our mission are tax deductible.

Wisdom Publications is affiliated with the Foundation for the Preservation of the Mahayana Tradition (FPMT).